D1014523

BRUSH UP YOUR

PIDGIN

DORGAN RUSHTON

ILLUSTRATED BY
WILLIAM RUSHTON

WILLOW BOOKS
Collins
8 Grafton Street, London
1983

A SENSIBLE, CONVERSATIONAL, BEGINNER'S PHRASEBOOK OF PIDGIN-ENGLISH

For The

BRITISH TRAVELLER

Including

AN EVERYDAY GUIDE TO SURVIVAL IN THE JUNGLES OF NEW GUINEA

NEW BRITAIN ★ NEW IRELAND
THE BISMARCK ARCHIPELAGO ★ NEW HEBRIDES
THE LOUISIADE ARCHIPELAGO
NEW CALEDONIA ★ THE SOLOMON ISLANDS
THE SANTA CRUZ ISLANDS ★ FIJI
& THE LOYALTY ISLANDS

Willow Books
William Collins Sons & Co. Ltd
London · Glasgow · Sydney
Auckland · Toronto · Johannesburg

First published in Great Britain 1983
© Text Dorgan Rushton 1983
© Illustrations William Rushton 1983

Stars page 109–116 by
David Fordham

Rushton, Dorgan
Brush up your pidgin
1. Creole dialects 2. Pidgin language – Terms and phrases
I. Title
417'.2   PM7802

ISBN 0 00 218021 9

Filmset by Rowland Phototypesetting Ltd
Bury St Edmunds, Suffolk

Printed in Great Britain by
St Edmundsbury Press, Bury St Edmunds, Suffolk

Pidgin-English

PISIN-INGLIS

Pidgin-English, usually referred to as Pidgin (Pisin), is an actual, extant language used by millions of people in the South Pacific. By means of this universal language, 600 different tribes, speaking 600 different languages, are able to communicate with each other.

Although at times Mrs Coffin's Pisin grammar and Pisin phonetic spelling are highly questionable, it would still be possible nowadays to use this Pisin phrasebook with a degree of confidence in any of the islands mentioned in the original title.

Take it with you anyway – the tropic-proof cover makes it an excellent all-weather hat.

Introduction

On 1 May 1933 Nicholas Ernest Coffin and his wife Daphne set out from Tilbury, England, on a voyage that was to take them to New Guinea. After many months at sea, gloriously chronicled in their book *Modern Travel From Ruislip to Rabaul* (published 1934, now sadly out of print), they arrived at New Guinea on 7 October 1933. Their brief: to write 'A Sensible, Conversational, Beginner's Phrasebook of Pidgin-English for the British Traveller'.

Back in Ruislip, Major Henry Latymer, ex-Army (gout) excitedly awaited the arrival of the first chapters, for he was to annotate the book and share his unequalled knowledge and experience of the jungle with their readers.

Sadly, at the time, the book was never completed. The intrepid pair disappeared off the face of the earth, thereby creating a mystery which has baffled the literary world ever since.

This year, the fiftieth anniversary of that doomed expedition, the Major, now 92 years of age and still living in Ruislip, has generously allowed us to see those documents, so painstakingly written in the depths of the jungle, carried by 'boys' through crocodile-infested rivers and snake-filled forests to the General Post Office in Rabaul, thence to be sent by boat halfway round the world to Ruislip.

Cast your mind back to 1933. On 5 December of that year the first chapters arrived on the Major's doorstep . . .

8

At Sea

LONG SODA WATER

Hello, sailor!	Halo, boscrew!
Good morning, captain!	Good moning, keptin!
Where are we, sailor?	You-me stop where, boscrew?
At sea, captain	Long soda water, keptin
Where's my medicine, boy?	Medecin belong me, where, boy?
In your hand, captain	Long han belong you, keptin
Hoist the mainsail!	Oistim sail!
Full speed ahead!	Orait, engin he run now!
I see Rabaul, captain	Me look-look Rabaul, keptin
I see three Rabauls, boy!	Me look-look trifella Rabaul, boy!
Look out, captain!	Lookout, keptin!
Good Lord! Slow the engine!	Yesus Kraist! S-l-o-o-o-w!
Steer straight for what's-its-name!	Shoot strait long what-name disfella place!
Go to starboard!	Steerboard!
Go to port!	Backboard!
Go straight ahead!	S-t-r-a-a-a-i-t!
Go about!!	Go boutim!!
GO BACK!!!	GO STEN!!!
I think the captain is drunk again, Daphne	Itingk keptin he long-long long wiski gen, Dapne

If the boat tips over, what will happen to the passengers, Nicholas?	Suppos bot he capsize, by-en-by all pasinga he make what-name, Nikas?
The sharks will eat them, Daphne	By-en-by all sark kisim all, Dapne
I do not feel well, Nicholas	Me feelim no-good, Nikas
I am seasick. I want the doctor!	Me sisik. Me likim dokta!
Where is the doctor?	Dokta, where?
The doctor is seasick, madam	Dokta he sisik, missis
Raise the anchor, boy!	Oistim upim anka, boy!
The anchor is raised, captain	Anka he oist-up, keptin
Bloody fool! I meant *drop* the anchor!	Bladiful! Me tok *leggo* anka!
Stop the engine!	Makim die engin!
There is no engine, captain	He no got engin, keptin
Bloody hell!	Bladi big-fire!
Gosh, Daphne, we have landed at Rabaul!	Oboy, Dapne, bot he fastin long Rabaul!
Help! Help!	Helap! Helap!
Man overboard!	Man long soda water!
What's the matter, Nicholas?	Wasamarra, Nikas?
The captain has fallen in the sea!	Keptin he fall-down long soda water!

NOTES (1933)

I'm a bit new to this writing business. Of course, I've written 'Regimental Orders, Other Ranks For the Use of' and that sort of thing, but that's not exactly Robinson Crusoe, is it? They told me I was to write a few notes and odd items of interest at the end of each chapter, so here goes.

I think it's all progressing reasonably so far. Young Nick and Daphne seem to be picking up the lingo quite well. Of course, they've yet to land and that's when it's really going to hit the fan.

Interesting about the captain. It sounds like old 'Windy' Green to me. If it was 'Windy', then he was drunk – no question about it. 'Windy' was always drunk. I've fallen into the drink with him myself on more than one occasion.

Fancy old 'Windy' still being alive. I can't get over it. He must have a liver like a fossilised football by now. He went native, you know. Chewed betelnut and married native gels. We always used to say he had a wife in every port bottle.

Funny chap, actually. One of his ears was eaten by the cannibals.

(Is this the sort of thing you want?)

--------- RECOMMENDATION ---------

If you're invited to the captain's cabin and the captain's name is 'Windy' Green,
KEEP YOUR LIFE JACKET ON!

Did I write this? I can't remember a word of it. Fifty years is a long time.
  New Guinea. I don't think it's even called that any more.

NEW WORDS

Well, they're all new words, aren't they? I'll try to pick out a few that may be of some use to you. You've probably noticed that there is no definite article, viz. 'the', in Pidgin. I think it makes it easier, really. None of that rubbish they have in French; I was always getting my sexes muddled at school. Now the indefinite article, viz. 'a', is 'wanfella' – one fellow. That's pretty simple, isn't it?

Long	Means in, at, on, to, from. Almost everything, really. It's in nearly every sentence, so we should deal with it right away. Normally, you have to work out which word it means, but luckily Daphne's done it for you.
Long-long	Nothing to do with the above at all. It means crazy, mad. So 'Long-long long wiski' means 'Out of his skull on whisky'. The more usual word for a drunk is 'spakman', but I think Daphne's is more poetic.
Kisim/gisim	Does not mean to kiss. It means 'to take' as in 'sark kisim' – the shark takes. Also used for 'give'. That one's a bit more complicated – we'll move on, shall we?
Belong	Obvious, isn't it? 'Mine' – belong me; 'yours' – belong you, etc.
By-en-by	By and by. This *always* indicates the future tense in Pidgin. So 'I will go' is 'by-en-by me go'. It's easy when you get the hang of it.

The rest looked pretty clear to me. What did you think?

The Arrival

COME-UP

Gangway!	You clear!
All right, Daphne, let's go!	Orait, Dapne, you-me go!
I think I am going to be sick again	Itingk sik he come-up long me wantime moa
Good heavens, Daphne!	Olapukpuk, Dapne!
Sorry, Nicholas. Sickness overcame me	Sory, Nikas. Sik he come-up long me
Why the hell didn't you throw up in the ocean, Daphne?	Watfor you no throw-out long soda water, Dapne?
I did not want to vomit on the captain	Me no like throw-out long keptin
Let's get away from here	You-me go
Hey, boy! Come here at once!	He, boy! Come here kwik-kwik!
Help me with my baggage!	Helapim carryim all someting belong me!
Good morning, sir. How are you?	Good moning, mista. You orait?
Hurry up, boy! It is very hot	Hariap, boy! He stop bladi hot
I am overheated and sweating profusely	Me too hot en plenty swet he come-up
It is about to rain, sir	Rain he like come, mista
Rubbish! The sun is beating down on me	Rabish! Sun he boinim me
Where is my wife?	Cook belong me, where?
Get a move on, Daphne!	Kwik-time, Dapne!

Hello, madam. How are you?	Halo, missis. You orait?
I am fine, thank you	Me orait, tenk you
I like small European women, madam	Me like lik-lik missis, missis
Thank you, boy	Tenk you, boy
Shut up, boy!	Sarap, boy!
All Americans are angry	All Amerikan belli hot
I am English, boy!	Me belong Inglan, boy!
All Englishmen are mad	All man belong Inglan he long-long
You know nothing, boy. You are brainless!	You savvy nutting, boy. You no got savvy!
I know how to count, sir	Me savvy countim, mista

1. WAN

2. TU

3. TRI

4. FO

8. HAIT

9. NAIN

7. SEWEN

10. TEN

6. SIKIS

5. FAIV

Daphne, did you write that down?	Dapne, you writim disfella?
Yes, Nicholas	Yes, Nikas
The small European woman has drawn a picture of me!	Lik-lik missis makim wanfella piksa long me!
We are writing a book, boy	Mefella writim wanfella book, boy
Golly, madam!	Oboy, missis!
Time is being wasted, Daphne	Time he lus nutting, Dapne
I have plenty of time, sir	Me got plenty time, mista
I haven't got plenty of time, boy!	Me no got plenty time, boy!
Where is my suitcase?	Beg belong me, where?
I do not know, sir	Aidono, mista
Find it, you lazy good-for-nothing!	Findim, you lazi buga!
I think your suitcase is in the ocean, sir	Itingk beg belong you he stop long soda water, mista
My suitcase is gone! I have lost my suitcase! I no longer have a suitcase!	Beg belong me he lus! Me lusim beg! Me no moa got beg!
Here it is, Nicholas! This is ours!	Him he stop here, Nikas! Him belong you-me!
It is raining, Nicholas. I am getting wet	Rain he come-down, Nikas. Me got water
Keep quiet, Daphne!	Finish tok, Dapne!
Boy! Put all my things in a heap	Boy! Bungim all someting belong me
Take this bag to the car	Kitchim disfella beg, takim long car

Take all:
  my bags
  my boxes
  my knapsacks
  my butterfly net
	Takim all:
	  beg
	  bokis
	  ruksack
	  umben belong bataplai } belong me

My ankle is broken, sir	Screw belong fut belong me he bugarup, mista
Bollocks!	Bol!

NOTES (1933)

Good show, Nicholas! I think, for a first time crack at it, he's done jolly well! By Jove, it's not easy dealing with those porter johnnies. I think young Nick struck exactly the right note: put him in his place and showed him who was boss.

Not much from the memsahib, but I know she was seasick and under the ship's doctor for most of the crossing. A very promising start.

Incidentally, I think this would be a good time to mention Daphne's little sketches. Plucky gel that: one minute she's throwing up, the next she's drawing. Of course, a lot of the sketches were in a pretty foul state when I received them, but I've managed to salvage a few and I think they should be included in the book.

Writing on its own can be awfully boring, don't you think?

——— RECOMMENDATION ———

The use of 'bastet' (bastard) when handling those blighters. 'Bol' (bollock/ball) is not the most effective word as it has no *exact* translation in English. Tu bol is possible, but not really recommended. Remember –

BASTET!

——— N·O·T·E·S (1983) ———

I'm not nearly so certain of this any more. Nowadays I think I'd plump for bollocks.

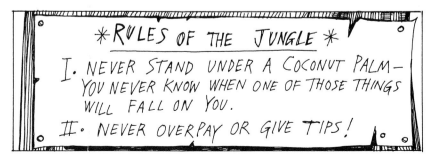

NEW WORDS

Can't see many here that aren't self-explanatory except:

screw belong fut	ankle
screw belong lek	knee
screw belong han	elbow/wrist
fingga	finger
fingga belong fut	toe
raithan	right hand
lephan	left hand

I know they're not all in the chapter but I thought I'd just throw them in.

On the Road

LONG ROT

Good morning, boss! I am your driver and your guide	Good moning, bos! Me driva en showman belong youfella
Where is our car, driver?	Car belong mefella, where?
Here, sir	Here, mista
This is a terrible car!	Disfella car he rabish car!
Yes, sir	Yesa
How old is the car?	Car he got how much Krismas?
Pretty old, sir	Plenty Krismas, mista
I want another car!	Me like urra-kind car!
Too bad, boss. The office is closed	Sory, mista. Ofis he fast finish
The Yam Festival is today, sir	Sing-sing Belong Mami he today, mista
I would like to go to the Yam Festival, Nicholas!	By-en-by me likim go long Sing-sing Belong Mami, Nikas!
That is not possible, Daphne	No can, Dapne
I will go with your daughter, sir	By-en-by me go wantime long pikinini mary belong you, mista
This woman is my wife!	Disfella mary he cook belong me!
Pretty old mister, madam	Plenty oldfella mista, missis
How much is it to go to the Ritz Hotel in Ralum, boy?	How much me payim you go long Rits Hotel long Ralum, boy?
That is too expensive!	He costim plenty money!

It's cheap, boss	He no costim plenty, bos
You want my second price, boss?	You like namba-tu pay belong me, bos?
Here, boy! I am not paying any more!	Here, boy! Me no payim moa!
All you New Guineans are robbers!	All youfella Nu Ginis man belong steal!
I like Americans, sir	Me likim all Amerikan, mista
I am not American!	Me no belong Amerika!
I know, boss	Me savvy, bos
You want to buy an umbrella, boss?	You like buyim wanfella ambrella, bos?
No, I do not!	No got, me no like!
I would like to buy an umbrella, Nicholas	Me like buyim wanfella ambrella, Nikas
Keep quiet, Daphne!	Fastin tok, Dapne!
I am getting very wet, Nicholas	Me wash-wash no-good, Nikas
My wife forgot the umbrella. The umbrella is in Ruislip	Cook belong me lusim tingk long ambrella. Ambrella he stop long Rislip
Get in the car, Daphne	Go long car, Dapne
You will dry on the journey	By-en-by you dry long driv
Start the car, driver!	Startim car, driva!
What is that smell?	What-name disfella smel?
The kerosene is leaking out, boss	Kerasin he lik, bos
What is that noise?	What-name disfella nois?
I think a screw is loose in the engine, boss	Itingk screw belong engin he lus, bos
(I think a screw is loose in the driver, Daphne)	(Itingk screw belong driva he lus, Dapne)

The roof is leaking, Nicholas	Ruf he lik, Nikas
The roof is not leaking on me, Daphne	Ruf he no lik long me, Dapne
Hey, maybe the small European lady would like to sit next to me, boss	Hey, itingk lik-lik missis like sindown close-to me, bos
Out of the question, driver!	No can, driva!
It is not far, Daphne	He no longway, Dapne
How far is it, driver?	How much longway, driva?

Sir, the hotel is:
 a great distance
 a fair distance
 some hours distant

Mista, hotel he:
 longway
 longway lik-lik
 longway too much

Are we going:
 north
 south
 east
 west?

You-me go:
 not
 sout
 sun he come-up
 sun he go-down?

I don't know, boss	Aidono, bos
At what time will we get to the hotel?	Watime by-en-by you-me come-up long hotel?
Between two o'clock and six o'clock, boss	Tu-klok he go finish, sikis-klok he no come-up yet, bos
Hello, the car has hit something!	Halo, car he bangim someting!
The driver has run over a pig	Driva he go-upim pik
Why has the driver stopped the car, Nicholas?	Watfor driva he stopim car, Nikas?
What on earth are you doing, driver?	What-name you makim someting, driva?
The pig is dead, boss. I am taking the pig home	Pik he die finish, bos. Me gisim pik long house belong me
You are stealing that pig, driver!	You stealim disfella pik, driva!

I didn't steal him, boss – I just took him	Me no stealim, bos – me gisim nutting
See, boss, he likes sitting in the car	Look-look, bos, he like sindown long car

You want a bit, boss:
    the leg
    the arm
    the head?
	You like lik-lik, bos:
	    lek
	    han
	    hed?

I cannot allow the pig to sit next to you, driver!	Me no can larim pik sindown close-to you, driva!
You want him next to you, boss?	You like him close-to you, bos?
Certainly not!	No got tru!
Start the car again, driver	Startim car gen, driva
Nicholas! The pig moved!	Nikas! Pik he make nois!
Come off it, Daphne	No got here, Dapne
I saw the pig move, Nicholas	Me look-look pik he make nois, Nikas
That was the flies, Daphne	He got all lang, Dapne
I feel sick, Nicholas!	Me feelim sik, Nikas!
Stop the car again, driver	Stopim car gen, driva
Please vomit at the rear of the car, Daphne	Pliz throw-out long arse belong car, Dapne
My wife is always vomiting	All-time all-time cook belong me he throw-out

NOTES (1933)

This is the chapter exactly as I received it. It comes to a rather abrupt end as Daphne continued to throw up and damaged the rest of it. However, sensible gel sent it on in a separate bundle.

The phrases in the other section are mostly concerned with paying the bill (as I expected, the driver demanded more money on their arrival at the hotel) and as this parcel was covered in mould when it reached Ruislip, I let it dry out then included it in another chapter entitled 'Useful Phrases when Paying the Bill'. That's coming up next, by the way.

To tell the truth, I'm a little worried by Daphne's behaviour. Oh, I know it's early days yet, but I'm wondering if she's going to stick it. You know, there are pigs all over the place out there and someone's always running over them. Ran over at least 50 myself. Old 'Peanut' McKenzie held the course record with 180. So, you see, Daphne's going to have to toughen up.

I'm disappointed young Nicholas didn't buy the umbrella. Elementary mistake, that. By golly, I was never without one the whole time I was there.

I remember what else I wanted to say. You know when the driver puts the pig in the car and offers Nick an arm? Perhaps you thought that was a mistake. Not so. To the natives the front legs of any animal are the arms and hands, and only the back legs are called legs. Sorry, I don't know why. Generous of him to have offered the head. I was surprised – the head is very highly prized.

RECOMMENDATION

Buy an umbrella and always carry it. If it doesn't rain (which is never), it is an invaluable weapon for dealing with natives, rats, etc., and can be put to good use removing run-over pig and that sort of thing. It's also handy in the jungle as a kitchen utensil, for stirring sago, barbecuing pig and so on.

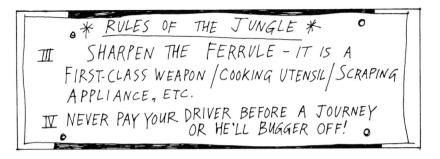

——— N·O·T·E·S (1983) ———

Nothing really.

NEW WORDS

The first one that probably strikes you as strange is:

Krismas	This means exactly what it says – Christmas. However, it is also used for almost any party or celebration at any time of the year. It also refers to age. 'How many Christmasses have you had?' is the only way to ask how old you are. God knows why.
Pikinini mary	A baby girl, a girl. Hence 'Pikinini mary belong you' – your daughter.
Pikinini man	Baby boy, a boy.
Monki	Teenager. There are no monkeys in New Guinea. (Be careful with this one, it also means someone's passive homosexual partner. Sorry if I've offended you.)
Cook belong me	I suppose you've gathered by now that this means wife. Wife can also be 'mary belong me'. 'Mary' refers to any woman.
Lusim tingk	Literally, to lose your thought; to forget. Thus 'Daphne forgot the umbrella' – Dapne lusim tingk long ambrella. (I suppose I should really go round and send it to them.)
What-name someting	What.

| Sing-sing | Means a festival, a dance, a singalong. Similar to Krismas, but more specifically to do with dancing and singing. |

Incidentally, there are festivals almost every day in Melanesia. The natives celebrate everything from yam planting (plantim mami) to funerals (plantim pipol).

That comment of the driver's about 'between two and six o'clock' is absolutely typical. So don't worry about it. They have no idea of time at all.

Useful Phrases
when Paying the Bill

GOODFELLA TOK LONG
TIME YOU PAY

I have no money!	Me no got money!
I have no more money!	Me no got moa money!
There must be some mistake!	Itingk he got rong!
Shut up or I'll box your ears!	Finish tok o you no finish tok me fightim hed belong you!
You are lying!	You giaman!
Your bucket is not full!	Buket belong you he no full-up!
Your boat has no paddles!	Bot belong you he no got pull!
Your bicycle has no bell!	Wil-wil belong you he no got belo!
I hope a fowl eats your rice!	Me hop wanfella kakaruk kai-kai rice belong you!
I hope the rice poisons your fowl!	Me hop rice gip kakaruk belong you!
I hope your yams die!	Me hop all mami belong you he die finish!
I hope your goat gets diarrhoea!	Me hop mare-mare belong you he pek-pek water!
I hope a crocodile eats your private parts!	Me hop puk-puk he kai-kai someting belong you!
I hope you get tinea!	Me hop you got grille!

NOTES (1933)

Daphne enclosed a rather gritty little note with this lot. I don't think she approves. She doesn't seem to realise that there's a certain cachet out there to thinking up a particularly fine insult. You can spend many happy hours in the jungle working out really splendid ones. They were always referred to as 'me hops'. One of the first things we'd say to each other was 'Heard any good "me hops" lately?'

I can still remember a prize 'me hop' attributed to 'Spotty' Bedson. I don't know whether it was actually his or not, but he used to shout it at the club when he wanted to clear the verandah of visitors. It went 'Me hop pik belong you gisim sik no-good long mumma en puppa belong you en he givim him long you en sista belong you!' (*I hope your pig catches a social disease from your mother and father and gives it to you and your sister!*)

It always made me laugh. Maybe it was the way he said it.

Funny old blighter, 'Spotty'. Well, he was until the cannibals ate his foot, then he got a bit morose. He still played a good game of bridge, but his golf handicap shot up. He came to a terrible end in '28. I don't even like to think about it.

Ah well, 'Spotty' has gone and Tempus Fugit.

Also remember:

BASTET!

(She's forgotten it again.)

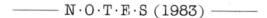

N·O·T·E·S (1983)

I'd forgotten that one of 'Spotty''s about the social disease. Nearly gave myself another hernia. Don't suppose it means much these days, though; you can only say those things in the privacy of your own home now.

NEW WORDS

Giaman	Now this word will be of particular interest to those of you who can still remember the Great War. The natives use it to describe a liar, a cheat, a blackguard and that sort of thing. We all knew it was a derivation of 'German' and probably dated back to their occupation of the country. So that is how we pronounced it – and particularly loudly when old 'Fritz' was at the bar.
Kai-kai	The Pidgin for food, a meal or eating.
Sista/brada	Looks easy, doesn't it? Obviously sister and brother. Well, it's so damned difficult I nearly didn't mention it. I'll try to get it right:

A man's brother is his brada and his sister is his sista. Now it gets more complicated. A woman's brother is her sista and her sister is her brada. I'm afraid cousins are also called brada and sista. Cousins of the same gender as the speaker are brada; of a different gender, sista.

I think, on the whole, it will be easier if you try to avoid becoming involved in local family life.

At the Hotel

LONG HOTEL

Good evening, sir. Welcome to the Ritz	Good ivning, masta. Hamamas long Rits
This is not an hotel, Nicholas!	Disfella he no wanfella hotel, Nikas!
Is this an hotel, boy?	Disfella place he hotel, boy?
Yes, sir	Yesa
There you are, Daphne!	He stop you, Dapne!
Do you have a room, boy?	You got wanfella room, boy?
Yes, sir. I have a hundred*	Yesa. Me got wan handet
My wife and I would like a room	Cook belong me en me likim wanfella room
Hello, madam. Have you had an accident?	Halo, missis. You gisim bugarup?
My wife has been ill	Cook belong me he throw-out
Remove the mess from your face, Daphne!	Take-awayim doti long face belong you, Dapne!
Where is your handkerchief?	Hankisip belong you, where?
Hurry up, boy! I would like to check in now	Hariap, boy! Me like gisim wanfella room now
I would like to check out!	Me like lusim room altagether!

*Wan handet: one hundred. The next morning Daphne counted the rooms at the hotel. There were three. The natives have a great deal of trouble with numbers. One hundred can mean anything, really. I had a native carrier once who told me that a new canvas bath would cost me about £500,023 0s 0d.

Shut up, Daphne!	Sarap, Dapne!
Please write your name in the book, sir	Pliz writim name belong you long book, masta
My name is blank	Name belong me blank
My age is blank	Krismas belong me blank
My address is blank	Adres belong me blank
The registration number of my alien card is blank	Namba belong alien cart belong me blank
I have blank children	Me got blank pikinini
Okay, Mr Blank, how long are you staying here?	Okei, Mista Blank, how much time you stop here?
Three nights, boy	Trifella night, boy
One night!	Wanfella night!
Be quiet, Daphne!	No tok, Dapne!
We are staying three nights	Mefella stop trifella night
On Friday we are going to the highlands	Fride mefella go long mounten on-top
I do not want to go to the highlands, Nicholas	Me no like go long mounten on-top, Nikas
The Major said we must go to the highlands, Daphne*	Maja tok you-me must go long mounten on-top, Dapne
There is a war on, sir	He got wan bigfella fight, masta

*Highlands: mounten on-top. Look here, this is absolutely awful! The lad's a fool! I never said 'You must go to the highlands', I said 'You must go to the _islands_'! I don't know what to do about it. Nothing I _can_ do, really. This chapter was posted two months ago. They must be there by now, if they went. I only hope someone had the sense to stop them. You see, there are ruddy great wars going on up there, non-stop, between some of the most savage tribes in the world. The hills are alive with cannibals. At weekends they are joined by the town natives who go along for a punch-up. It's no place for a white man, I can tell you.

I think I need a drink.

Bloody fool! The war ended in 1918!	Bladiful! Fight he finish long 1918!
We are very tired, boy	Mefella tired too much, boy
We would like a double room, at the double!	Mefella likim wanfella room belong tufella, kwik-kwik!
I would like a single room, Nicholas	Me likim room belong wanfella, tas-all, Nikas
I am becoming cross, Daphne!	Me kross, Dapne!
Mr Blank, every three persons must share a bed and a blanket	Mista Blank, trifella trifella he must sleep long wanfella bed unerneat wanfella blanket
Rubbish, boy! My wife and I want a double room with a bath and a lavatory	Rabish, boy! Cook belong me en me like wanfella room belong tufella wantime long place wash-wash en place pis-pis
There are no rooms with lavatories, sir	He no got room wantime long place pis-pis, masta
Where is the lavatory, boy? Is it upstairs?	Place pis-pis, where, boy? He stop on-top?
There is no upstairs, sir	He no got on-top, masta
Is it downstairs?	He stop down-belo?
There is no downstairs, sir	He no got down-belo, masta
The lavatory is at the bottom of the garden, sir	Place pis-pis he stop long arse belong garden, masta
The other side of the pig-pen, sir	Urra-side place belong pik he stop, masta
I want to go home, Nicholas!	Me like go long house belong me, Nikas!
That's enough, Daphne!	He stop inuf, Dapne!
How much is the room for a day, boy?	How much long room long wanfella day, boy?
That is too expensive!	He stop too dear!

Where is the nearest inexpensive hotel?	Hotel stop close-to him no dear too much, where?
There are no other hotels, sir	He no got urra-fella hotel, masta
I see. Right, where is the dining-room?	Me savvy. Orait, room kai-kai, where?
The dining room is closed, sir . . . the Yam Festival	Room kai-kai he fast finish, masta . . . Sing-sing Belong Mami
I know it's the damn Yam Festival, boy!	Me savvy demim Sing-sing Belong Mami, boy!
Don't shout, Nicholas!	You no big-mouse, Nikas!
Shut up, Daphne!	Fastin mouse, Dapne!
Why the hell are you crying, Daphne?	Watfor you cry, Dapne?
What is the matter?	Wasamarra?
Do stop crying, Daphne!	Stopim cry, Dapne!
Give me my key, boy	Gisim key belong me, boy
There is no key, sir	He no got key, masta
We need a key to lock the door, you silly ass!	Mefella likim key long lockim dor, ful!

There is no door, sir	He no got dor, masta
Bloody hell!	Bladi big-fire!
Right! Where is the bloody bedroom?	Orait! Bladi room belong sleep, where?
The bedroom is down the hall, sir	Room belong sleep he stop down small room belong hangim-upim coat en het, masta
Next to the goat stall	Close-to house mare-mare he stop
Follow me, sir	Come behind long me, masta
Be careful where you tread, sir!	Lookout where you putim fut, masta!
For God's sake, Daphne, blow your nose!	Bladishit, Dapne, windim nos belong you!
You stupid woman! Why are you always crying?	Kranki mary! Watfor you cry-cry all-time?

NOTES (1933)

Now Daphne has started to cry and if I know women, and I don't very well, once they've started to cry it's like rising damp – bloody hard to stop. They tend to go potty in the tropics, you know. We all had a lot of bother with them. 'Porker' Johnson's wife cried for five years.

It did occur to me that Daphne might be sickening.

I can remember Ralum in the '20s. By Jove, what a place! The Ritz had an upstairs then. I spent my leaves there in '24, '25 and '27. Always had the top right-hand room. Of course, judging from Daphne's sketch, it's not there any more, but I've crawled up those stairs many a time.

We used to hold goat races around the billiard table and one night old 'Shorty' McKay got so arseholed he sat under the table and proposed to the winner. Said she had the best tits (susu) on the island. 'Porker' said it was because he'd finally found someone his own size. I must confess he was pretty short, hence the name. I've written 'sat under the table' up there, but now I'm wondering if he wasn't standing under the table.

The district commissioner stationed at Ralum then was a nice Australian chap, drank a bit, called 'Fish' Codd, and he performed the marriage. We dressed the bride in curtains and flowers and found a top hat for 'Shorty'. After the ceremony, the groom passed out and the bride ate the bouquet.

Dirty Mary (Doti Mary) ran the place then and, despite her personal habits, she didn't make a bad job of it. Every Saturday (Satde) there was a thé dansant *(ti sing-sing)* at the hotel and people came from miles around. There was a native orchestra the missionaries had taught to play, so interspersed with the popular tunes we'd get the odd Abide With Me but on the whole they were very smart affairs indeed. Shaving was de rigueur. Not for the ladies, of course.

I have a dance programme somewhere and an old photograph of a thé dansant in the Ritz ballroom. Would they be of any interest, do you think?

Thé Dansant
Dance Programme
Saturday, 12 July 1925

The Ritz Hotel
Ralum

Your hostess: Mrs M. McGarrity

1 Abide With Me *(Tango)* ....
   (SINDOWN WANTIME LONG ME)

2 To Be A Pilgrim *(Polka)* ....
   (WALKABOUT EN PRE)

3 All Things Bright and Beautiful *(Barn dance)* ....
   (ALTAGETHER SOMETING NAISFELLA)

4 Onward Christian Soldiers *(Military two-step)* ....
   (UNERARMS ARMI BELONG KRAIST)

5 God The Omnipotent *(Charleston)* ....
   (GOT SAVVY TOO MUCH)

6 Hills of The North, Rejoice *(Quickstep)* ....
   (MOUNTEN BELONG NOT, LARF)

7 The Day Thou Gavest, Lord, Is Ended *(Waltz)* ....
   (DAY YOU GIVIM, GOT, HE DIE FINISH)

8 Hymn 87 *(Valeta)* ....

Music provided by: **Admission: 2/6**
'The Holy Band of Unfortunates' from   (including tea and cakes)
the leper colony of the Big Sisters of the Rich

If you're going to the tropics, don't get married. If you do, make sure she doesn't cry and vomit.

N·O·T·E·S (1983)

Of course, I've never been married, so it's easy for me.

NEW WORDS

I can't see any difficulties here, though I do think it's a good idea to give you the other days of the week:

Monday	Mande
Tuesday	Tude
Wednesday	Wenesde
Thursday	Tesdi
Friday	Fride
Saturday	Sarere/Satde
Sunday	Sande

This might be a good time to give you the months of the year, in case they omit those too. The months have simplified English names but are usually referred to as Namba-wan Moon, Namba-tu Moon, etc.

Namba-wan Moon	Yanuari	Namba-sewen Moon	Yuli
Namba-tu Moon	Febuari	Namba-hait Moon	Augus
Namba-tri Moon	Mars	Namba-nain Moon	Setemba
Namba-fo Moon	Epril	Namba-ten Moon	Oktoba
Namba-faiv Moon	Mai	Namba-ten-wan Moon	Nowemba
Namba-sikis Moon	Yuni	Namba-ten-tu Moon	Disemba

The only other things I can see you having trouble with are:

Wantime long   Always used for 'with'.

Unerarms (songsheet)   'Under arms'. Literally, to charge.

I can't see any others.

PLACE BELONG
GO OUT

In the Bedroom

LONG ROOM BELONG SLEEP

Here is the bedroom, sir!

Place sleep he stop here, masta!

Make the bed, boy!

Makim bet, boy!

I have already made it, sir

Me all-right-him finish, masta

This place abounds in mosquitoes

Disfella place he full-up long gnat-gnat

Close the window to keep out the mosquitoes, boy

Fastin windo, no-good all gnat-gnat he come inside, boy

There is no window, sir

He no got windo, masta

Is there a mosquito net?

He got wanfella kalamboo?

Put the mosquito net over the bed!

Tightim kalamboo, fastin kalamboo!

Boy! Get me:
    a clean towel
    soap
    toilet paper

Boy! Gisim me:
    wanfella clean taol
    sop
    toilet pepa

I would like some disinfectant, Nicholas

Me likim poisin belong kilim germ, Nikas

I think you mean deodorant, Daphne

Itingk you tok medecin belong makim bodi smel nais, Dapne

Sorry, sir. I have not got everything

Sory, masta. Me no got altagether someting

Goodnight, sir. Goodnight, madam

Goodnait, masta. Goodnait, missis

Daphne, my darling!

Dapne, you leva belong me!

I am very tired, Nicholas	Bun belong me he hevy, Nikas
I have a headache	Hed belong me he pain
My dress is ruined	Klos belong me he bugarup
I would like a new dress, Nicholas	Me likim newfella klos, Nikas
What for, Daphne?	Watfor, Dapne?
It is very expensive to buy new dresses!	Costim plenty money buyim all newfella klos!
Iron your dress, Daphne, it will be fine	Ironim klos belong you, Dapne, by-en-by he makim moa beta
You never give me anything, Nicholas!	You no got wanfella time givim me wanfella someting, Nikas!
Don't start that again, Daphne!	You no startim disfella gen, Dapne!
Heat the water for my bath, wife!	Hotim water belong wash-wash, cook belong me!
The hot water is not hot yet	Hot water he no hot yet
The hot water is cold	Hot water he kol
There is no more water	He no got moa water
Where is the manager of this place?	Bosboy belong disfella place, he stop where?
I have a complaint!	Me got tok!
I will telephone him	By-en-by me telipon him
There is no telephone, Nicholas	He no got telipon, Nikas
Right! Get the bed ready, Daphne!	Orait! Rediim bet, Dapne!
There is a crocodile under the bed, Nicholas!	He got wanfella puk-puk unerneat bet, Nikas!
He has been dead for a long time, Daphne	Hed belong him he stink finish, Dapne
There is a dog under the bed, too	He got wanfella dok unerneat bet, too

Beware of the dog, Daphne!	Lookout long dok, Dapne!
The dog is under the bed to frighten rats	Dok he stop unerneat bet belong makim frait all rat
Nicholas! The dog has eaten my hat!	Nikas! Dok he kai-kaim het belong me!
My hat is on my head where it belongs, Daphne	Het belong me he stop long hed belong me where him belong, Dapne
There is a spider on my pillow, Nicholas!	He got wanfella spaida long pilo belong me, Nikas!
It is an enormous spider	Him he bigfella spaida
That is no spider, Daphne. That is a cockroach, that's all	Disfella he no spaida, Dapne. Disfella he wanfella kokoros, tas-all

Daphne, where is:
    the toothbrush
    the toothpaste
    the comb
    the shaving cream
    the hairbrush
    the talcum powder?

Dapne,
    brus belong clean tiit ⎞
    paste belong clean tiit ⎟
    kom   ⎟
    krim belong shevim ⎬ where?
    brus belong grass ⎟
    talkum pouda ⎠

I don't know	Aidono
Daphne, I am undressing, my sweet one!	Dapne, me lusim lap-lap, you swit biskit!
You are unattractive and past your prime	You dry biskit
Pardon?	Sory?
Nothing, Nicholas	Someting nutting, Nikas

Daphne, hang up my clothes in the cupboard:
    my shirt
    brown trousers
    grey trousers (the money
      stays in the pocket,
      Daphne)

    short trousers
    pair of drawers

Dapne, hangar-upim klos belong me long kabod:
    siot belong me
    trousis all-same ground
    trousis all-same shit
      belong fire (money he
      stop long beg belong
      trousis, Dapne)
    sotfella trousis
    anderwear

singlet	singlis
pullover	pulova
braces	bresis
shoes	shu
socks	sokin
hat	het
panties	penti
petticoat	unerneat-skert
stockings	longfella sokin
blouse	blaus
brassiere	baskit belong titti
girdle	godle

Heavens! There is a pig in the cupboard!	Heven! He got wanfella pik long kabod!
I think it belongs to the crocodile	Itingk him he belong long puk-puk
The crocodile is alive, Nicholas	Puk-puk he got laif, Nikas
The crocodile has bitten the pig!	Puk-puk he kai-kaim pik!
The crocodile is disembowelling the pig!	Puk-puk he rausim belli belong pik!
The dog smells the meat	Dok he smelim abus
What shall we do?	What-name you-me makim someting?
Quickly, get into bed!	Kwiktime, go long bet!
Alone at last, Daphne!	You-me tas-all Dapne!
Good evening!	Good ivning!
Good God! Who are you?	Good Got! Who's-at?
I am the third man under the blanket	Me trifella man he must sleep unerneat blanket
Why did you let my pig out of the cupboard?	Watfor you lusim pik belong me long kabod?

NOTES (1933)

A pig is very important in New Guinea. If you should come across one in a cupboard – leave it there! There will always be some good reason for its being there.

Now, I know I'm not here to criticise Nick or Daphne, but I must point out that the exchange between Nicholas and 'the third man under the blanket' would have been a good deal more pleasant if young Nick had not started with 'Good God! Who are you?' A simple 'Good evening to you, too' ('Good ivning long you, too') would have been more appropriate. 'How are you?' or 'Are you all right?' would have been equally acceptable.

In a footnote to me, Daphne said that she could not continue writing as the lantern had been knocked over by the animals, but that she, personally, was not at all dismayed by this unexpected meeting with one of the locals. Later, she tried to make up for Nick's ungracious behaviour and, I'm glad to say, she was amply rewarded. After all, as she pointed out, the fellow was a guest of the hotel, a fellow guest of theirs, and a guest in their bed. Under the circumstances, it seemed perfectly natural to try to get on with him.

Daphne's attitude is commendable. Unfortunately, we all know that Nicholas has a very short fuse.

It's important to remember that crocodiles always look as if they're dead unless they're moving. When they're moving it's too late to realise they're not dead.

---------- RECOMMENDATION ----------

SHOOT THE BUGGERS!

--------- N·O·T·E·S (1983) ---------

I think this is still pretty sound advice. Don't think I can improve on it at all. Of course, I haven't seen a pig in a cupboard for years.

(Mrs P. wouldn't allow it.)

NEW WORDS

Someting nutting

Now this is interesting. It's used *ad nauseam* by the natives, usually accompanied by a shrug. It means not important, nothing, a trifle – that sort of thing. 'Him he someting nutting' means 'that's nothing'.

All

Simply denotes the plural. 'All' in Pidgin is 'altagether'.

Something else that hasn't come into the chapter, but I'd like to mention it now I remember it, is the matter of a native's reply to a negative question. This can be very confusing to the traveller but it follows the most important rule in Pidgin: be logical. Hence we get:

You didn't see him, did you?   You no lookim him?

Yes (I didn't see him)   Yes

You didn't go today, did you?   You no go today?

Yes (I didn't go today)   Yes

It's better English, really, don't you think?

At Breakfast

LONG KAI-KAI

Stop scratching, Daphne. The waiter is coming	Stopim skrap, Dapne. Kukiboy he come now
Good morning, sir	Good moning, mista
We would like a table, waiter	Mefella likim wanfella tebal, kukiboy
This table is too small	Disfella tebal he lik-lik too much
I want a larger table	Me likim wanfella tebal he bigfella moa
There aren't any, sir	He no got wanfella, mista
This table is wet!	Disfella tebal he got water!
Yes, sir. It is raining	Yesa. Him rain
Well, get a move on, boy!	Orait, hariap, boy!
We want breakfast	Mefella like kai-kai now
Daphne! I said stop scratching!	Dapne! Me tok stopim skrap!
Hello, madam	Halo, missis
Good morning, waiter	Good moning, kukiboy
How are you this morning, madam?	You orait today, missis?
I'm fine, thank you, waiter. I am very well indeed	Me orait, tenk you, kukiboy. Me orait too much
You were very fine last night, too, madam	You orait too much long yesti-nait, too, missis

Good heavens! You are the third man under the blanket, waiter!	Goodfella heven! You trifella man he stop unerneat blanket, kukiboy!
Yes, madam	Yes, missis
How nice to see you again!	How much naisfella look-look you wantime moa!
I say, waiter, stop waffling on! Where is the newspaper?	Me tok, kukiboy, you stopim tok! Niuspepa, where?
I want a newspaper double-quick	Me likim wanfella niuspepa kwik-kwik
You want it to smoke, boss?	You like him belong smok, bos?
You want it for the lavatory, boss?	You like him belong go long place pek-pek, bos?
I want it to bloody read, boy!	Me like him belong bladi riitim, boy!

No newspaper today, sir. The newspapers come:
    tomorrow
    the day after tomorrow
    two days after tomorrow
    three days after tomorrow
    sometime
    never
	He no got niuspepa today, mista. All niuspepa come-up:
	    tomorra
	    half tomorra
	    half tomorra moa
	    half tomorra moa yet
	    samtime
	    he no got wanfella time

Let me see the menu, boy!	Me like lookim all disfella kai-kai, boy!

Right! I want:
    coffee in a coffeepot
    tea in a teapot
    chocolate milk
    instant coffee
    hot chocolate
    two soft boiled eggs
 	
    two hard boiled eggs
 	
    two scrambled eggs
 	
    two eggs sunnyside up
	Orait! Me likim:
	    kofi long kofipot
	    ti long tipot
	    soklet milik
	    kwik kofi
	    hot soklet
	    tufella kio all he no
	        boilim strong
	    tufella kio all he
	        boilim strong
	    tufella kio all he
	        makim wantime batta
	    tufella kio all
	        suniside up

two eggs once over lightly	tufella kio all he capsizim kwik-kwik by-en-by arse belong him come-up on-top
Goodness me! That is a really different meal, sir! (The man is insane!)	Oboy! Disfella he urra-kind kai-kai, mista! (Man he long-long!)
Hurry up, boy! I am hungry	Hariap, boy! Me hangre
My wife is hungry	Cook belong me hangre
Are you sir's wife, madam?	You cook belong mista, missis?
What a pity! I am in love with another man's wife!	Kalapa! Me mangaal mary belong urra-fella man!
Does madam want coffee?	Missis likim kofi?
Yes please, darling	Yes pliz, you leva belong me
Waiter! We are in a hurry	Kukiboy! Mefella he hariap
I want my eggs *now*!	Me likim all kio belong me *now*!
Don't shout, Nicholas!	You no big-mouse, Nikas!
The waiter has gone to the kitchen	Kukiboy he go long house kuk
Take off your hat at the table, Nicholas	Takawayim het long hed belong you long tebal, Nikas
My hat is keeping me dry, Daphne	Het belong me he makim me dry, Dapne
The galvanised iron roof has a hole in it	Kafa he got ole
I would like to buy an umbrella, Nicholas	Me like buyim wanfella ambrella, Nikas
You have an umbrella in Ruislip, Daphne	You got wanfella ambrella long Rislip, Dapne
Good gracious, Daphne! Where are your shoes?	Olaman, Dapne! Shu belong you, where?
The goat ate my shoes, Nicholas	Mare-mare he kai-kaim shu belong me, Nikas
I would like new shoes, Nicholas	Me likim newfella shu, Nikas

Hold on now! You don't need shoes, Daphne	You wet now! You no likim shu, Dapne
The natives don't wear shoes. You will have nice, cool feet, Daphne	All kanaka he no cartim shu. By-en-by you got all naisfella fut he col, Dapne
Waiter! Where is my coffee?	Kukiboy! Kofi belong me, where?
Coming, sir!	He come now, mista!
Waiter, pour the coffee in my cup	Kukiboy, capsizim kofi long cup belong me
Waiter! Where the hell are my eggs?	Kukiboy! Westat all kio belong me?
Look out, blockhead! You have spilt the eggs!	Lookout, kukhed! You capsizim all kio!
Now the eggs are all over my wife	Now all kio coverupim cook belong me
And I have a little on my shoe!	En me got lik-lik long shu belong me!
Clumsy idiot! We English like to eat off a plate	Krankiman! All mefella belong Inglan likim kai-kai long plet
I am so sorry, madam. Sir bumped me	Me sory too much, missis. Masta sakim me
You cheeky bugger!	You big-mouse buga!
Please allow me, madam	Pliz larim me, missis
Waiter! Stop playing with my wife's bosom!	Kukiboy! Stopim pilay long susu belong cook belong me!
He is removing the egg, that's all, Nicholas	Him he takawayim all kio, tas-all, Nikas
Don't throw away the egg on your stomach, Daphne. Put it on my plate	You no troiim kio long belli belong you, Dapne. Putim him long plet belong me
The egg smells awful, Nicholas	Kio he stink, Nikas

Waiter! I want a:
    fork
    knife
    spoon
    shovel
	Kukiboy! Me likim wanfella:
	    fook
	    nife
	    spun
	    sovel

Daphne! I have broken a tooth!	Dapne! Me bugarupim wanfella tiit!
A button off your dress was in my egg!	Wanfella baton belong klos belong you he stop long kio belong me!
Where is the dentist?	Doktatiit, where?
There is no dentist, sir. However, there is a witchdoctor in the village	He no got doktatiit, mista. He got dokta belong poisin long village, tas-all
I don't want the bloody witchdoctor, you ignorant savage!	Me no like bladi dokta belong poisin, you bush kanaka you long-long!
I am not a savage, sir	Me no bush kanaka, mista
And he is not ignorant, Nicholas	En he no long-long, Nikas
Shut up, Daphne! How would you know?	Sarap, Dapne! How much you savvy?
It is raining again	Rain he come-down wantime moa
My bloody eggs are getting wet	All bladi kio belong me he got water

NOTES (1933)

There weren't any holes in the roof in my day. I can't stand the thought of wet eggs myself and, what's more, I never had them, thanks to my trusty brolly. Here's a wrinkle I picked up out there:

Always eat under your umbrella in the jungle

1. *Select an area.*
2. *Clear it of snakes, leeches, ants, spiders, etc.*
3. *Place your mosquito net over your umbrella.*
4. *Raise the umbrella above your head.*
5. *Unfurl the umbrella.*

You now have a handy, portable shelter for all your meals. It keeps out sun, rain, flies, mosquitoes and bird droppings and can be easily held in place by a few pebbles should there be a hint of wind. Needless to say, it does an absolutely first-class job as an outhouse (the same rules apply. Just be particularly vigilant re the spiders, etc.) I also found it a most sensible way to walk through the jungle. I admit it did tend to catch on the

undergrowth, but it's well worth it to get away from the bloody flies. In any case, I'm quite a dab hand with the old needle. As a matter of fact, over the years I became rather well known for this mode of travel and the natives used to call me 'The Walking Tent' ('Shithaus He Go Walkabout').

Where was I? Ah, yes. Good to hear Daphne say she's feeling fine again. Obviously a night with her feet up has done the trick.

Speaking of feet, I'm none too keen on her going around barefoot. It's most ill-advised; the ground abounds with hookworm, snakes, insects and the like.

And I must say I don't think much of that breakfast menu. What about:

liver	leva
kidney	kidni
pork chops	half pook
mutton chops	slais miit belong seep-seep
sausage	sosis
sliced bacon	slais beiken

I'm sure there was a better selection in Dirty Mary's day. On second thoughts, I'll say a wider selection. I've just remembered 'Dirty''s stab at a kedgeree for a gala breakfast on the King's birthday and to this day I don't know what went on in the making of it. To begin with, it was grey. Secondly, it smelt pretty awful (and I haven't got much of a sense of smell – it's been a godsend all my life). Thirdly, on closer inspection, it appeared to be full of cigarette butts, cigar ends, bits of cane chair, hair and what looked like fingernails. I slipped mine to one of the pigs who, interestingly enough, wouldn't look at it. Unfortunately, old 'Four Eyes' Robinson had already eaten his. Poor chap developed nicotine poisoning and damn near died.

'Four Eyes' always considered himself a bit of a ladies' man and some weeks later this new woman arrived in town. It was past sundown after one of 'Dirty''s thé dansants, and we were all pretty squiffy. Anyway, 'Four Eyes' takes her shoe, fills it with gin and socks it back. The thing was she'd put a good deal of talcum powder in the shoe (a wise precaution in the heat).

Now, what with the powder floating on the top and the odd bits of fluff and grass, it looked quite vile sloshing about. Though not to 'Four Eyes' of course, who was blind as a fruit-bat. He downed it, as I said, in one, gave her back her wet shoe and died three days later.

Sorry about that, it's rather a sad story.

―――― RECOMMENDATION ――――

1. *Do* put talcum powder in your boots.
2. Do *not* drink out of them.

By the way, Daphne was right about that egg. It still smelt when it reached Ruislip and rather alarmed the postman, long suffering though he is.

―――― N·O·T·E·S (1983) ――――

You know, reading all this and looking back over the years has been a revelation to me. I sometimes wonder if I was completely sane in those days.

NEW WORDS

Now we all know about Nick's short fuse but he really shouldn't have called the waiter a 'bush kanaka'. This means a hillbilly or, as Daphne puts it, an ignorant savage.

Don't call a native a 'bush kanaka'. It's the way to a sudden end.

At the Post Office

LONG HOUSE POST

Where is the post office, boy?	House post, where?
I am the post office, sir	Me stop post ofis, mista
Come under the umbrella, sir	Come unerneat long ambrella, mista
Where can I mail these parcels?	By-en-by me salim all disfella parsol, where?
I have two parcels and two letters here	Me got tufella parsol en tufella pas here
I want to send them to England	Me like him go long Inglan
They are going to Major Latymer in Ruislip	By-en-by all disfella he go long Maja Latymer long Rislip
Not 'The Walking Tent', sir!	Him he 'Shithaus He Go Walkabout', mista!
Certainly not!	No got tru!
Give me the necessary stamps for these packages, boy	Givim me samfella stemp long all disfella parsol, boy
I would like a postcard, Nicholas	Me likim wanfella poskart, Nikas
Not now, Daphne	No can now, Dapne
What is inside these parcels, sir?	What-name someting he inside long all disfella parsol, mista?
A book, boy	Wanfella book, boy
These parcels are damp, sir	All disfella parsol he col, mista
It is raining, boy	Rain he come-down, boy

I smell sago, sir. Are you exporting sago?	Me smelim sak-sak, mista. You salim sak-sak?
Of course not!	No got!
I can smell egg, too, sir	Me can smelim kio, too, mista
Why are you sending eggs to England, sir?	Watfor you salim all kio long Inglan, mista?
I am not sending eggs to England!	Me no salim all kio long Inglan!
My wife has had several accidents	Cook belong me he gisim samfella bugarup
I can see that, sir	Me savvy look-look, mista
How much will I have to pay, boy?	By-en-by me payim long how much, boy?
You want first-class mail or you want second-class mail, sir?	You likim namba-wan mail o you likim namba-tu mail, mista?
What is the difference?	What-name someting he urra-kind?
First-class mail – I run. Second-class mail – I ride the bicycle	Namba-wan mail – me run. Namba-tu mail – me go long wil-wil
I want to send them the cheapest way	Me like salim all go, tas-all, me no like payim plenty money too much
You want second-class, sir	You likim namba-tu, mista
How much is that?	How much long disfella?

Paying the Bill.

Why is this woman writing down everything I say?	Belong what-name disfella mary writim altagether someting me tok?
Is the lady from the government office?	Mary belong long ofis belong gavman?
We are writing a book, boy	Mefella writim wanfella book, boy
Am I in the book, sir?	Me belong long book, mista?
Yes, if you don't speak too quickly	Yes, suppos you tok isi
I must learn to read	Me must lernim riitim
Did I say good things, madam?	Me tok goodfella tok, missis?
Yes, thank you	Yes, tenk you
I like small European women, madam	Me likim lik-lik missis, missis
That's enough, boy! We are going now	Him tas-all, boy! Mefella go now
Goodbye sir, madam. I must hurry to Rabaul	Goodbai mista, missis. Me hariap go long Rabaul

63

I am going to the highlands on Friday	Fride, me go long mounten on-top
The village is fighting away on Saturday	Satde, disfella place he fight long mounten
We are going to the highlands, too, boy!	By-en-by mefella go long mounten on-top, too, boy!
For the war, sir?	Belong fight, mista?
For the book, boy!	Belong book, boy!
Come, wife, I am now penniless	Come, cook belong me, me rabishman now
I must go to the bank immediately!	Me must go long benk wan-tu!
I would like some money, Nicholas	Me likim samfella money, Nikas
What on earth for, Daphne?	Watfor, Dapne?

NOTES (1933)

It's interesting, isn't it? Here is the very conversation they had with the postmaster in Ralum nearly two months ago, and here are those self-same letters and parcels on my front porch in Ruislip. (Mrs P. won't let them in the house.)

I'm not at all sure now that Ralum was the right place to send Daphne and Nicholas. It seems to have changed a good deal since I was there. Of course, things disintegrate very quickly in the jungle. People, too.

There was a proper post office in Ralum in the old days. When I say 'proper', I mean it had four walls and a roof. I think it had a roof. Certainly had three walls, anyway. Perhaps it burned down. Then, again, perhaps Daphne's little sketch is more artistic than accurate. I'm no judge. I mean on the artistic side; there's nothing artistic about me at all.

RULE

X. THE JUNGLE IS
NO PLACE
FOR ARTISTIC PEOPLE

N·O·T·E·S (1983)

I think this is a little unfair. Obviously I was in a bate at the time. Nowadays, I can't see any reason why artistic people shouldn't go to the jungle.

NEW WORDS

Wil-wil   Wheel-wheel, hence bicycle. Easy, isn't it?

Isi   Easy. 'Tok isi' – talk slower

I had a quick flick through but this was all I could find. Rather encouraging, that.

At the Bank

LONG BENK

Right, boy! I would like some money!	Orait, boy! Me likim samfella money!
So would I, sir	Me too, mista
Hello, missis!	Halo, missis!
I don't think you understand, boy! I would like to cash a cheque	Itingk you no savvy, boy! Me like gisim money long wanfella chek
So would I, sir. Hello, missis!	Me too, mista. Halo, missis!
Pay attention! This is a bank, isn't it?	Atenson! Disfella he benk?
Yes, sir. This is a bank	Yesa. Disfella he benk
But it's not a very good bank, sir	Him he no goodfella benk, tas-all, mista
It has no money	He no got money
Then why the hell are you here, boy?	Orait, watfor you stop here, boy?
I sell umbrellas, sir	Me selim all ambrella, mista
Then give me the money from selling the umbrellas	Orait, gisim me money belong selim all ambrella
I haven't sold any yet, sir	Me no selim wanfella yet, mista
You want to buy an umbrella, missis?	You like buyim wanfella ambrella, missis?
If you buy an umbrella, missis . . .	Suppos you buyim wanfella ambrella, missis . . .

then I can give the money to sir	orait, me can givim money long masta
The boy's a bloody fool, Daphne!	Boy he bladiful, Dapne!
Hello, missis!	Halo, missis!
That's it! I don't want to hear any more!	Ass-it! Me no like hearim wanfella someting moa!
Stop writing, Daphne!	Stopim writ, Dapne!

NOTES (1933)

Now this is more like it! The post office, I mean. I wonder if Daphne has muddled the two. You see what I mean: three walls and a roof. I'm sure she has them confused. If that's the case, though, what's happened to the bank? I remember it well: 'Ralum Benk – Youfella Putim, Mefella Holdim'.

Of course, it wasn't very popular. For some reason the natives pool their money each week and each week a different fellow gets the lot. Never understood how it worked or why they all did it, except that when one's turn came up it must have been like winning a sweepstake. (Not that all the wages in New Guinea ever amounted to much.)

Speaking of money, they use the same monetary system as we do, but the names are mostly German. Why should Germany represent mammon? God alone knows.

3d	threepence	lik-lik mark
6d	sixpence	half mark
1/-	one shilling	mark
10/-	ten shillings	bigfella mark
£1	one pound	money kunda

You will have noticed the curious fact that there is no Pidgin word for penny. This always caused a great deal of hilarity on the club verandah whenever one of the newer ladies would declare that she was just going 'to spend a penny'. 'Not in New Guinea!' we'd all cry, much to her amazement.

N·O·T·E·S (1983)

I suppose they've gone metric now, like the rest of the world.
   Ruislip metric. Never thought I'd live to see the day.

NEW WORDS

No new words, you'll be glad to hear.

As there aren't any, I thought I'd take the opportunity to pop this in, even though it has nothing to do with anything. Except Pidgin, that is:

XI.

HOW TO BECKON IN PISIN

(a) EXTEND THE ARM TO ITS FULL LENGTH
(b) PUT HAND OUT WITH PALM DOWN
(c) JERK THE HAND BACK TOWARDS YOURSELF
(d) WAIT PATIENTLY – OCCASIONALLY JERKING.

DO NOT DRINK AND TRY TO TALK PIDGIN

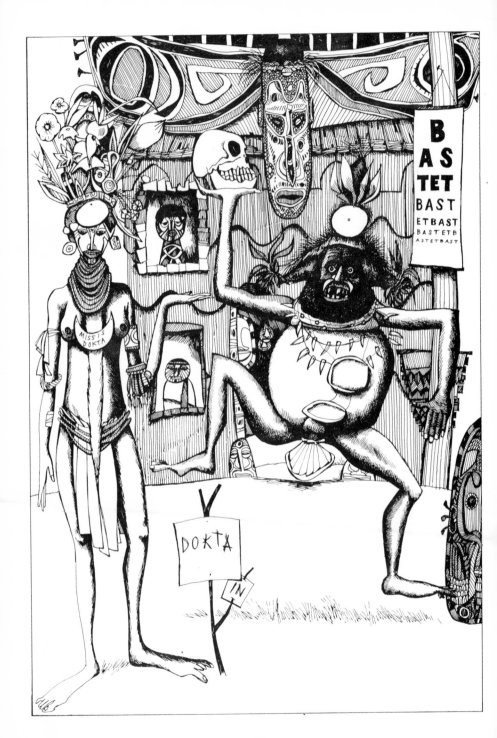

70

At the Doctor's Surgery

LONG HOUSE BELONG DOKTA POISIN

Good afternoon, doctor	Good avinun tru, dokta
Please don't interrupt your dance, doctor	Pliz you no stopim sing-sing, dokta
I am finished now, lady	Me finish now, missis
I have put a spell on the mud men	Me putim wanfella poisin long all man belong ground he-got-water
Now we will win the fight on Sunday!	Now mefella by-en-by winim fight long Sande!
I thought the fight was on Saturday, doctor?	Itingk fight he long Sarere, dokta?
Bloody sheet! I'll have to do it again!	Bladishit! By-en-by me must makim someting gen!
I like small European women, lady	Me likim lik-lik missis, missis
Thank you, doctor	I enk you, dokta
What can I do for you, lady?	What-name someting, missis?
My husband has broken his tooth	Man belong me he bugarupim wanfella tiit belong him
Oh good! I like teeth!	Goodfella! Me likim tiit!
See my nice dog-tooth necklace, lady?	You look-look long naisfella dok-tiit belong me, missis?
I will put your husband's tooth on my necklace	By-en-by me putim tiit belong man belong you long dok-tiit belong me

Where is the tooth, lady?	Tiit, where, missis?
And where is the husband?	En maritman, where?
My husband has gone!	Man belong me he go finish!
You want me to put a spell on him, lady?	You likim me putim wanfella poisin long him, missis?
He'll die pretty quick	By-en-by he die finish kwik-kwik

NOTES (1933)

I don't know, I'm a little disappointed with this chapter. I can't understand it, there used to be a dentist and a proper doctor in Ralum when I was there. I can't believe this is going to be of any use to the British traveller, but you will need to know the following:

diarrhoea	pek-pek water
dysentry	pek-pek blad
constipation	no savvy pek-pek
orchitis	bol he swell-up
rheumatism	all screw he pain
insanity	long-long
fracture	bun he broke
gonorrhoea	klep
fever	skin he hot

All of them everyday occurrences in the jungle.

Our dentist was old 'Foul Mouth' Ferret who surprised us all by running off with 'Porker''s wife. They were last heard of at a place called Bulli in Australia, which sounds as if the residents have pretty strong stomachs and probably no teeth left, which is just as well.

I remember bumping into 'Foul' at the club one lunchtime and he was so drunk he didn't know who I was. Then it transpired he didn't know who he was, either. He was usually pretty far gone by that time of day, so none of us ever made appointments with him in the afternoon. At any time, he had terminal halitosis and most of us preferred to pull our teeth with a door. Well, you can't very well use a gas mask at the dentist's, can you? When there was general laughter at the bar, our mouths looked like unkempt cemeteries. Amazing about Mrs 'Porker'. She must have had even less sense of smell than me.

Our doctor, old 'Septic' Saunders, had a first-class cure for diarrhoea which is worth a mention here. He'd discovered it in India. It was called Indian Brandee and we used to down it by the bucketload. By George, it was good stuff.

His wife, I think she was called Beatrice (she was an ex-actress. 'Septic' used to complain she was more ex than act), used to cook with it. Cause, effect and cure all at the same time. I know – I've eaten there. You wouldn't believe what she could do with a tongue sandwich.

—— N·O·T·E·S (1983) ——

Do you know, for 50 years now I've been trying to lay hands on some Indian Brandee. For 30 years I asked our chemist in Ruislip, old Boot, to try to get some in, then he died. Silly old bugger, I bet you he never even tried. And for the last 20 years I've been asking his son, young Boot, if he'd oblige. For 20 years the idiot has been smiling and nodding and patting me on the head. I'll bet you he hasn't tried, either. He'll be the next to go, you'll see. The man's a fool to himself.

NEW WORDS
Once more – no new words.

At the Department Store

LONG BULK STOR

Welcome to the department store, sir and madam	Hamamas long bulk stor, mista en missis
Come in! Admission free! No charge for looking!	Comon! Come inside nutting! No payim belong look-look!
I sell everything!	Me selim altagether someting!
You need a raincoat, madam?	You likim wanfella coat-rain, missis?
Could you speak slower, please, Mr Shopkeeper?	You tok isi, pliz, Mista Storman?
I am trying to write it all down	Me tryim writim altagether someting you tok
You writing another book on Pidgin-English, madam?	You writim wanfella book moa belong Pisin-Inglis, missis?
Yes, I am	Yes, me savvy
I am in all the books, madam	Me stop long altagether book, missis

I say 'Would you like to buy a:	Me tok: 'You like buyim wanfella:
wireless	wailis
mosquito net	kalamboo
frying pan	fraipen
grass skirt	pur-pur
hurricane lamp	lamp walkabout
kerosene lamp	kerasin lamp
corkscrew	op botol he got screw
bottle opener?' and they put it in the book	op botol?' en all putim him long book

This will be a different book, boy!	Disfella book by-en-by he urra-kind book, boy!

They all say that, sir	All altagether tok all-same youfella, mista
Enough of this! Let us talk business	Inuf-o! You-me tok bisnis
We would like to see some frocks, boy	Mefella likim look-look samfella klos, boy
Nicholas! Are you buying me a new frock?	Nikas! You buyim me newfella klos?
Of course, my dear	Yes, swit biskit
May I try one on?	Inuf me tryim wanfella?
That one is too tight, Daphne	Disfella he tight too much, Dapne
I think it is too loose, Nicholas	Itingk he bigfella too much, Nikas
That one is too short, Daphne	Disfella he sotfella too much, Dapne
I think it is too long, Nicholas	Itingk he longfella too much, Nikas
Nicholas, this one is lovely!	Nikas, disfella him goodfella tru!
My wife would like a hat to go with the frock, boy	Cook belong me likim wanfella het belong klos belong him
Nicholas! Are you buying me a hat, too?	Nikas! You buyim me wanfella het, too?
Find a hat for my wife, my man!	Findim wanfella het long cook belong me, bosboy!
Nicholas, do you like this one?	Nikas, you likim disfella?
I like only pink hats, Daphne	Me likim all ping het, tas-all, Dapne
My wife also needs a pair of good shoes	Cook belong me likim wanfella per goodfella shu
Nicholas, that is too expensive!	Nikas, disfella he dear too much!

Do you have any sandals?	You got sendal?

What colour would you like, madam:
    red
    yellow
    white?
	What-name coller you like, missis:
	    ret
	    yelo
	    wait?

I like these shoes, Nicholas	Me likim disfella shu, Nikas
Would you like anything else, Daphne?	You likim altagether someting, Dapne?
I would love an umbrella, Nicholas	Me likim too much wanfella ambrella, Nikas
Certainly, Daphne. Fetch an umbrella for my wife, my man!	Orait, Dapne. Gisim wanfella ambrella long cook belong me, bosboy!
Thank you very much, Nicholas	Tenk you too much, Nikas
Now I think I would like to buy a new suit for myself	Now itingk me like buyim newfella soot belong me
I like a conservative style	Me likim kind-kind style belong all man belong bifor
I prefer a double-breasted suit	Me likim dobel-bres soot
These trousers are too tight in the seat	Disfella trousis he tight too much long arse
Can you let them out?	Inuf you lusim out?
Is this the biggest size you have?	You got bigfella size?
Do you have a tweed sports jacket, boy?	You got spot jeket long ruf wool, boy?
This one is fine!	Disfella he goodfella tru!
You want it, sir?	You like him, mista?
I'll think about it	By-en-by me tingk-tingk long him

Do you have any bathing costumes?	You got samfella kostum belong wash-wash?
Nicholas, could we have terry-towelling bathing robes, too?	Nikas, inuf you-me gisim tery klos gown belong wash-wash too?
Of course, Daphne	Yes, Dapne
God bless you, sir!	Got blesim you, mista!
As you are buying these things, sir . . .	Suppos you buyim disfella someting, mista . . .
then you get a free ticket to the concert today	orait you gisim wanfella tikit costim nutting go long konset today
I can give madam a free appointment with the hairdresser, too	Me can givim missis wanfella tanget costim nutting wantime long man belong cutim grass belong all mary, too
Here are your tickets!	Tikit belong youfella he stop here!
Would you like anything else, sir? A:	You likim altagether someting, mista? Wanfella:
refrigerator	bokis ais
axe	akis
the kitchen sink?	tub?
Daphne, would you like some:	Dapne, you likim:
lipstick	lipstik
face powder?	fes pouda?
I would like:	Me likim:
a mild laxative	medecin belong pek-pek
something for a toothache	wanfella belong tiit pain
Immediately, sir!	Wan-tu, mista!
Right, my man, that's the lot!	Orait, bosboy, tas-all!
I am so happy, Nicholas	Me hepi too much, Nikas
Are you taking these things now, sir?	You takawayim all disfella someting now, mista?
Certainly not! We are not buying these clothes, boy!	No got tru! Mefella no buyim all disfella klos, boy!

We are writing a book on buying clothes, that's all	Mefella writim wanfella book belong buyim all klos, tas-all
You can wrap the laxative and something for my toothache	You can coverupim someting belong pek-pek en wanfella belong tiit pain belong me
Daphne! Put down that axe!	Dapne! Putim down disfella akis!
Daphne, remember the book!!	Dapne, holdim long tingk-tingk long book!!
You want to buy the axe, madam?	You like buyim akis, missis?
It is very cheap	He no costim plenty

NOTES (1933)

By Jove, they did really well with this chapter! It's all there; I don't have to add a thing. Except perhaps a warning about swimming anywhere in New Guinea:

DON'T DO IT!

The rivers are full of crocodiles and the sea is full of sharks. So don't bother about a bathing costume. (I think the phrases concerned with buying one are misleading. We don't want our traveller to come home legless, do we?)

I was constantly at the bulk stor myself, mostly to pick up mosquito netting and needles and thread. In the club they used to say if I was ever lost they could follow the trail of torn netting to find me. They called it my 'Old Man's Nuisance' and 'Spanish Beard' and said that the place would look more like the Everglades than N.G. by the time I left.

The bulk stor was a veritable treasure trove. I remember fossicking about in there one day and coming across some knitting needles and an old pattern book, so I set to and taught myself to knit. Unfortunately, it happened to be a pattern book for babies' bootees and, after I'd mastered them all, I had a devil of a job knowing what to do with nine odd bootees. They ended up on my golf clubs. (We'd carved this two-hole golf course out of the jungle. Course record: 'Jumbo' Patterson – 17. It would have been less but he lost his ball on the second green.) They looked so jolly with their ribbons dangling that I started knitting them for the other chaps, too. During my time in New Guinea I successfully completed 193 bootees.

But I digress. I was telling you about my quick turnover in mosquito nets. One of the reasons I needed so many was the damned cassowaries. Now, I don't know if you're familiar with the cassowary, but it's a fearsome bird: over five feet tall, claws like razors and an unpleasant disposition. I found the old umbrella an excellent defensive weapon but, frankly, I recommend shooting the buggers. Once you've shot them it's up to you whether you eat them or not. I preferred 'or not'. Their flesh is black, most unappetising and tough as old rope.

I was out motoring with old 'Peanut' one day (a five-pig trip) when we had an argy-bargy with a tree and had to walk back to Ralum. 'Peanut' was in a pretty vile temper as he'd wanted to push up his pig score. 'Foul Mouth' had hit seven the previous day and they were neck-and-neck. So 'Peanut' was banging away at anything that moved. He'd shot six snakes, a few flying foxes and the odd gekko when we were viciously set upon by two rampaging cassowaries.

One slashed away at 'Peanut' and sent his gun spinning off into the undergrowth, while the other ripped my mosquito net to ribbons. As usual, I was ready with my umbrella but, by golly, he was strong. Nearly knocked it out of my hand several times. A very sticky situation, I can tell you. The cassowary is known to be responsible for at least 20 deaths a year.

What is of particular interest, I think, is our method of escape. Since the cassowary can't fly, we climbed a tree. There we stayed for five hours in all until old 'Fish' and his boy (don't know what his name was – we always called him 'Chips') motored past, saw torn netting everywhere, stopped and rescued us. And that's it, really. All I can say is:

RULE OF THE JUNGLE N° XIV.

BE WARY OF THE CASSOWARY

Speaking of car accidents, something I should have mentioned earlier is that, should you have one, or get stuck in the mud, or break down, never ask a native to give you a 'push'. 'Push-push', 'pushim' and 'pusim' all mean 'to copulate' and the natives, being very amenable people, will do as requested. I hope I'm not too late with this warning. Sorry, I've only just thought of it. One of our early padres, 'Hellfire' Harrison, made this

elementary blunder when his Morris got bogged down on the old Rapopo road. The poor chap had to be put on the next boat home. By night. Under a blanket. Whinnying, I believe.

While I'm on the subject, 'go-upim' can also mean 'to copulate', but you're not as likely to get into trouble with this one.

I was just glancing through the manuscript and that bit about the 'kerosene lamp' caught my eye. Reminded me of one of my favourite phrases in Pidgin: 'Eclipse' is 'Kerasin lamp him belong Yesus Kraist him bugarup finish altagether'. I don't think I'll be pre-empting anything Daphne might write. There's not due to be an eclipse in New Guinea for two years.

———— N·O·T·E·S (1983) ————

While we're on favourite phrases, here are two of Daphne's: violin (it looks like a piece of wood and when the lady takes another stick and scratches its belly it makes a noise like a cat); and piano (a big box inside he has lots of teeth like a shark and when the lady hits it and kicks it he makes a great deal of noise).

'Foggy''s wife was round the other day and she mentioned one of her favourites: 'Helicopter' in Pidgin is 'Mix masta belong Yesus Kraist'. Of course, there weren't any helicopters in my day. Mrs P. told me not to put it in as she doesn't 'get it', but then she wouldn't, would she?

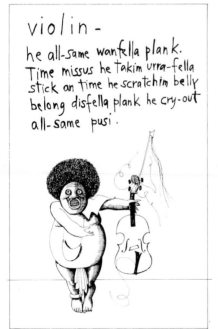

violin -
he all-same wanfella plank.
Time missus he takim urra-fella
stick on time he scratchim belly
belong disfella plank he cry-out
all-same pusi.

piano -
Wan bigfella bokis
inside he got plenty tiit
all-same sark an time
missus he hitim an kickim he
cry out too much.

NEW WORDS

I'm not doing any more New Words.

At the Hairdresser

LONG PLACE BELONG MAN CUTIM GRASS BELONG ALL MARY

Hello, sweetie!	Halo, switi!
Hello, are you the hairdresser?	Halo, man cutim grass belong all mary he you?
Yes, honey. My name is – Jesus Christ!	He tru, honi. Name belong me – Yesus Kraist!
Pardon?	Me no hearim
My God, sweetie! I just saw your hair!	Got Belong Me, switi! Me look-look long grass belong you!
You poor thing!	Me sory long you!
You look like something the cat dragged in!	You all-same someting pusi he bringim inside!
I know. May I have a shampoo?	Me savvy. Me likim wanfella sempu?
Oh dearie, yes!	O sory, he tru!
I have a free ticket here	Me got wanfella tikit costim nutting here
Goodness me, you must have bought a lot of things at the department store, sweetie	Oboy, you buyim plenty someting long bulk stor, switi
The proprietor is my friend	Storman he monki belong me
That's nice	Naisfella
No! I hate him	No got! Me haitim him
I'm sorry. Could I have a shampoo and set?	Me sory. Me likim wanfella sempu en wanfella set?

Anything, sweetie! Would you like:	Altagether someting, switi! You likim:
your hair cut	cutim grass belong you
your hair bleached	blitzim grass belong you
your eyebrows plucked	pulim eyegrass belong you
a pedicure	cleanim en washim en cutim fut
a manicure	cutim en sharpim en cleanim fingga-nil
a permanent wave?	rippel he stop longtime?
This is a hairdressing school	Disfella he skool belong cutim grass belong all mary
I am the teacher, sweetie	Me titsa, switi
Hurry up, girls! Look at this! We have a small European person here. Bring the bona bona bucket!	Hariap, all mary! Look-look long disfella! You-me got wanfella lik-lik missis here. Bona buket he come!

NOTES (1933)

Now I think he could well be artistic. Daphne has done extremely well, but I feel I should redress the balance and put down a few phrases for the men, with one proviso: be cautious of the native with a razor in his hand! Remember: they are all cannibals at heart and not to be trusted, no matter how artistic they seem.

(Mrs 'Septic' told me that it is all to do with their diet. Too many vegetables. And sago is renowned for having no vitamins whatsoever. That's why they eat people. They do eat whites but I believe they prefer to eat each other. Don't let this lull you into a false sense of security, however. At our annual get-togethers in Ralum we were always being mistaken for inmates of the leper colony, we had so many bits missing.)

Back to the phrases:

Could I have a shave?	You shevim me?
I want a haircut	Me like you cutim grass belong me
Cut it short, please	Cutim sot, pliz
Use the clippers	Usim klippa
Trim my moustache	Cutim mousegrass belong me
No 'Odour of Violets'	Me no like 'Smel belong Vailet'

—— N·O·T·E·S (1983) ——

Short hair is a thing of the past now. My barber in Ruislip has let his clippers rust.

At the Concert

LONG KONSET

Your hair is terrible, Daphne	Grass belong you he rabish, Dapne
I like it, Nicholas	Me likim him, Nikas
Stop crying, Daphne!	Stopim cry, Dapne!
Your nose is running	Nos belong you he got kus
Could you get me a Coca-Cola, Nicholas?	Inuf you givim me wanfella Koko-Kola, Nikas?
No, Daphne. The concert is starting now	No can, Dapne. Konset he bigin now
Are you ready, Daphne?	You redi, Dapne?
I have broken my pencil, Nicholas!	Me bugarupim pensil belong me, Nikas!
I need a pencil sharpener	Me likim mashin belong sharpim pensil
They are talking too fast, Nicholas!	All tok-tok kwik-kwik too much, Nikas!
Keep quiet, Daphne. I can't hear	Sarap, Dapne. Me no can hearim

Julius Caesar
YULI SEEZA

Friends, Romans, countrymen, lend me your ears

Frend, all man belong Rom, wan-tok, hearim me now

I come to bury Caesar, not to praise him

Me come long plantim Seeza, no tok-tok good long him

The evil that men do lives after them

Someting no good belong all man stop behind time he die

The good is oft interred with their bones

Someting good he plantim wantime long all bun

So let it be with Caesar

Maski Seeza too

The noble Brutus hath told you Caesar was ambitious

Bigfella Brutus tokin you long Seeza he mangaal

If it were so, it was a grievous fault

Suppos all-same, bigfella pekato tru

And grievously hath Caesar answered it

En Seeza he tok backim finish

Here, under leave of Brutus and the rest

Here, bikos all he givim me orait

For Brutus is an honourable man

Tru, Brutus he goodfella man

So are they all, all honourable men

All frend belong him goodfella man too

Come I to speak in Caesar's funeral

Me come tok-tok sory long plantim Seeza

He was my friend

Him he frend belong me

Faithful and just to me	Goodfella, goodfella tas-all long me
But Brutus says he was ambitious	Brutus callim him mangaal, tas-all
And Brutus is an honourable man	En Brutus he goodfella man too
He hath brought many captives home to Rome	Him he bringim plenty man belong calabus long Rom
Whose ransoms did the general coffers fill	By-en-by money belongim makim money belong ofis gavman full-up
Did this in Caesar seem ambitious?	All-same what-name? Seeza he mangaal?
When the poor have cried, Caesar hath wept	Time rabishman cry-cry, Seeza too him sory en cry
Ambition should be made of sterner stuff	Mangaal he got moa
Yet Brutus says he was ambitious	Tas-all Brutus callim him mangaal
You all did see that on the Lupercal	Time belong Lupercal youfella lookim
I thrice presented him a kingly crown	Trifella time me like makim king
Which he did thrice refuse	Trifella time he givim back
Was this ambition?	You lookim. Him he mangaal?
Yet Brutus says he was ambitious	Tas-all Brutus callim all-same
And sure, he is an honourable man	Orait, him he goodfella man
I speak not to disprove what Brutus spoke	Aidono, Brutus. Me no like tok no good long Brutus. Me no like kross him

But here I am to speak what I do know	Tas-all me tok-tok long someting here someting me savvy tru
You all did love him once, not without cause	Longtime bifor youfella likim too much bikos him strait
What cause withholds you then to mourn for him?	Watfor you no can sory long him now?
Oh judgement! Thou art fled to brutish beasts	O court! Anyway, youfella all-same wilepik
And men have lost their reason	No got savvy. Belli belong you full-up long kapok, tas-all
Bear with me. My heart is in the coffin there with Caesar	You wet lik-lik. Hat belong me he stop long bokis here wantime long Seeza
And I must pause till it come back to me	En me wet lik-lik bifor hat belong me come back long me wantime moa
Author! Author!	Come-upim book! Come-upim book!
Good God, Daphne! Is that all you wrote?	Goodfella Got, Dapne! You writim disfella, tas-all?
I'm sorry, Nicholas. I told you my pencil was broken	Me sory, Nikas. Me tok pensil belong me bugarupim
Would you let me use your fountain-pen?	You larim me usim founten-pen belong you?
Certainly not. You might break it, too	No can. You can bugarupim him, too
Here is my pencil, Daphne	He got pensil belong me, Dapne
Give it back when you've finished with it	Time you finishim, givim him back

90

The actor is talking again, Daphne!	Showman tok wantime moa, Dapne!
Write this down!	Writim disfella!
He called out: 'Altogether now!'	Him he singout: 'Altagether now!'
They are singing *God Save The King*, Daphne	All he sing-sing *Got Standby Long King*, Dapne
Why aren't you standing up, Daphne?	Watfor you no standap, Dapne?

GOT STANDBY LONG KING

Got standby long King,
Standby long King belong me,
Standby long King.

Givim big-name long all,
Stop good, en winim all,
Longtime King, tas-all,
Standby long King.

My pencil, please, Daphne	Pensil belong me, pliz, Dapne

NOTES (1933)

Never got on with Shakespeare myself. Do you think this is of general interest, or do you think we should scrap it? There aren't too many fellows running round the jungle spouting Shakespeare, I can tell you.

God Save The King should stay, of course, but that might make a rather short chapter. We could put in another song we used to sing in the bar of the club nearly every night. We learnt it from the natives, who called it Homesickness (Me Cry Long House Belong Me) and for some strange reason it is set to the music of Drink To Me Only With Thine Eyes. To hear the strains of Drink To Me Only echoing through the jungle just before sun-up with the birds just beginning their daily racket used to turn my stomach.

ME CRY LONG HOUSE BELONG ME

Place belong me he namba-wan,
Me likim him tas-all,
Me tingk long puppa, mumma too,
Me cry long house belong all.

Me work long place he longway tru,
Me stop no-good tas-all.
Place belong me he namba-wan,
Me likim him, tas-all.

(I always used to think of Ruislip when I sang it.)

HOMESICKNESS

My home town is the best home town,
I love it best of all,
I think of my father, my mother too,
I'm homesick for them all.

I work in a place that's a long way away,
I'm not happy about it at all.
My home town is the best home town,
I love it best, that's all.

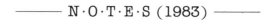

N·O·T·E·S (1983)

Just sitting here in Ruislip singing it over to myself. Funny thing – when I sing it now I think of Ralum.

At the Coconut Grove

LONG LINE KOKONAS

This is the famous Coconut Grove, Daphne	Disfella he Line Kokonas he got big-name, Dapne
The Coconut Grove is the best restaurant on the island	Line Kokonas he namba-wan house kai-kai long ailan
Good evening, sir! Hello, small European woman!	Good ivning, mista! Halo, missis!
Waiter, we would like a table for two	Kukiboy, mefella likim wanfella tebal belong tufella
(See page 51 – At Breakfast – re tables)	
The dining room is very crowded, waiter	Room kai-kai he full-up plenty man, kukiboy
It is the Sago Festival, sir	Him he sing-sing Belong Sak-sak, mista
All the men are having a big party	Altagether man he makim bigfella Krismas
Tomorrow the Ralum army goes to war	Tomorra armi belong Ralum he go fight
Waiter! This tablecloth is extremely dirty! Take it away!	Kukiboy! Disfella lap-lap belong tebal he doti altagether! Takawayim!
A dog is sitting under the table, Nicholas	Wanfella dok he sindown unerneat tebal, Nikas
That is not a dog, Daphne. That is a rat	Disfella he no dok, Dapne. Disfella he rat
I have no shoes on, Nicholas	Me no got shu, Nikas
Stop complaining, Daphne	Stopim tok, Dapne

After the Show...
Why not Dine at The Coconut Grove?

Waiter! Why the hell are you standing idle! Lay the table!	Kukiboy! Watfor you stop nutting? Lainim plet!
I like small European women, madam	Me likim lik-lik missis, missis
Shut up, waiter!	Fastin mouse, kukiboy!
This place is full of flies, Nicholas	Disfella place he got plenty lang, Nikas

Shut up, Daphne!	Sarap, Dapne!
Waiter, I want:	Kukiboy, me likim:
tinned meat	tin mit
(in the tin)	(long tin)
(on the plate)	(long plet)
chopped lizard	gekko he krungutim
owl in a basket	taragau he flai long nait
	long baskit
boiled cassowary	muruk boilim
shark stew	sark muk-muk
Lancashire hot possum	cus-cus belong Lankisir he
	hot
tree kangaroo meat balls	kapul bol
ratatouille	rat en mami
snake tartare	snek he no tan too much
Kentucky fried fingers	all fingga belong Kentuki
	he fryim
sweet potato	kau-kau
sago pancakes	sak-sak fryim
sago pudding	sak-sak hot water
roast sago	sak-sak muk-muk
chocolate sago	soklet sak-sak
strawberry sago	strooberi sak-sak
papaya sago	popo sak-sak
pie à la Mode	pai à la Style
I would like a little soup, waiter	Me likim lik-lik sup, kukiboy
And do you have fresh fish?	En you got newfella pis?
We have only sago, sir	Mefella got sak-sak, tas-all, mista
Waiter! Waiter! There is a fly in my sago!	Kukiboy! Kukiboy! He got wanfella lang long sak-sak belong me!
No, sir, there are two flies mating in your sago	No got, mista, he got tufella lang he push-push long sak-sak belong you
Would you like to dance, Daphne?	You likim sing-sing, Dapne?
You know dancing is my delight, Nicholas	You savvy me likim sing-sing, Nikas

Daphne! I have stepped in something on the floor!	Dapne! Me krungutim someting long ground!
It is the rat's mess, Nicholas	Him he pek-pek belong rat, Nikas
My shoes smell foul, Daphne	Shu belong me smel no-good, Dapne
You're telling me!	Now what-name!
Waiter! Bring: the pudding the afters	Kukiboy! Gisim: puding kai-kai behind
Hey, small European lady! You want to go for a walk with me?	Hey, lik-lik missis! You likim go walkabout wantime long me?
What did the waiter want, Daphne?	Kukiboy, he likim what-name someting, Dapne?
He asked me for: cigarette paper an empty box a mousetrap	Him he askim me long: smokpepa wanfella bokis nutting wanfella plank belong lik-lik rat
I think you are lying!	Itingk you giaman!
The waiter is a flirt and a bigmouth, Daphne	Kukiboy he humbugman all-same big-mousen, Dapne
He is a charming young man, Nicholas	Him he switfella all-same yongfella, Nikas
Waiter! I have a complaint!	Kukiboy! Me got tok!
Waiter! Waiter! There is a cockroach in my sago!	Kukiboy! Kukiboy! He got wanfella kokoros long sak-sak belong me!
Yes, sir. To eat the flies	Yesa. Kai-kaim all lang
Why the hell are you two laughing?	Watfor youfella larf?
Stop laughing immediately!	Stopim larf wan-tu!
Nicholas! You have spilt my drink	Nikas! You capsizim dringk belong me
The tablecloth is all wet	Lap-lap belong tebal he got water altagether

Take it off!	Bringim he go!
My dress is all wet!	Klos belong me he got water altagether!
Take it off, madam	Lusim him, missis
Shut up, waiter!	Sarap, kukiboy!
I will get you a tablecloth, madam	By-en-by me gisim you wanfella lap-lap belong tebal, missis
I am going to the lavatory, Daphne. You stay here	Me go long place pek-pek, Dapne. You stop here
Where's the lavatory, waiter?	Place pek-pek he stop where, kukiboy?
It is behind a tree in the Bush	He stop behind wanfella tri long Bush
Beware of the snake, sir!	Lookout long snek, mista!

Here, madam, I have a tablecloth!	Here, missis, me got wanfella lap-lap belong tebal!
You want to go for a walk now, madam?	You likim walkabout now, missis?
You can take off your dress in the Bush	By-en-by you can lusim klos belong you long Bush
And you can put on the tablecloth	En by-en-by you putim lap-lap belong tebal long you
Thank you, waiter	Tenk you, kukiboy
That is a beautiful moon, waiter	Disfella he naisfella moon, kukiboy
Moonlight becomes you, madam	Moon he light makim you naisfella too, missis
I love your hair, madam	Me likim too much grass belong you, missis
Would you like a cigarette, madam?	You likim smok, missis?
I have no cigarettes, waiter	Me no got kapstan, kukiboy

I have cigarettes, madam	Me got smok, missis
My heart beats. I yearn for you, madam	Hat klok belong me he make nois. Me mangaal long you, missis
Have another puff, madam	You like smok wantime moa, missis?
Yes, thank you, darling	Yes, tenk you, you swit biskit

Daphne! Hello! I am back from the lavatory!	Dapne! Halo! Me come-back long place pek-pek!
Where is my wife?	Cook belong me, where?
Where is the waiter?	Kukiboy, where?
I saw a small European lady and a waiter walking in the Bush, sir	Me lookim wanfella lik-lik missis en wanfella kukiboy walkabout long Bush, mista
They were passing a cigarette one to the other	All he eraboutim kapstan
They were singing, sir	All sing-sing, mista
That was no small European lady; that was my wife!	He no got lik-lik missis; he got cook belong me!
There are no flies in my sago now	He no got wanfella lang long sak-sak belong me now
There are eight cockroaches	He got hait kokoros

Hello, Nicholas, old bean! Did you find the lavatory?	Halo, Nikas, oldfella bin! You findim place pek-pek?
Daphne! Take those flowers out of your hair!	Dapne! Takawayim all disfella pul-pul long grass belong you!
Where is your frock?	Klos belong you, where?
Where the hell have you been?	Westat you go?
I was in the Bush watching a tiger, Nicholas	Me walkabout long Bush look-look bigfella wilepusi, Nikas
There are no tigers in New Guinea, Daphne	He no got wanfella wilepusi long Nu Gini, Dapne

He escaped from the zoo, Nicholas	He ronaway long bigfella garden belong putim longtime all wile someting he savvy walkabout long Bush, Nikas
Good God! Are you drunk, Daphne?	Goodfella Got! You spakman, Dapne?
No, Nicholas	No got Nikas
Then why are you laughing?	Watfor you larf?
Because I just wrote 'No got Nikas', Nicholas	Bikos me writim 'No got Nikas', Nikas
And I have no knickers, Nicholas	En me no got penti, Nikas
Slut! Bitch!	Pamokmary! Dok mary!
Bad language is not allowed here, sir	All tok no-good he tamboo here, mista
Get out, pea-brain!	You raus, kukhed!
I am writing all this down, Nicholas	Me writim altagether someting you tok, Nikas
What bloody page are we on now?	You-me stop long what-name bladi page now?
I don't know. Nearly at the end of 'Dining Out'	Aidono. Close-to finish 'Kai-kai Long House Kai-kai'
Here is your bill, sir	Disfella pepa he singout long pay belong wanfella someting you buyim finish, mista
Are you drunk, too, waiter?	You spakman, too, kukiboy?
Will you pay now, sir?	You payim now, mista?
I have put your betelnuts in a bag, madam	Me sakim bilinat belong you, missis
Will you take a cheque, waiter?	You gisim wanfella chek, kukiboy?

No, sir. We want:
    three pigs
    two goats
    one wife
	No can, mista. Mefella likim:
	    trifella pik
	    tufella mare-mare
	    wanfella cook belong you

You bastard!	Bastet!

(See page 29 – 'Paying The Bill'.)

Are you coming back tomorrow, madam?	Tomorra you come-back, missis?
Tomorrow we are going to the highlands, waiter	Tomorra mefella go long mounten on-top, kukiboy
Me too, madam! Are you coming with us in the aeroplane?	Me too, missis! By-en-by you come wantime long mefella long balus?
I suppose so. Do you know a good hotel in the highlands?	Itingk. You savvy wanfella hotel he goodfella long mounten on-top?
There are no hotels in the highlands, madam	He no got wanfella hotel long mounten on-top, missis
You must stay with my family, madam	By-en-by you must stop wantime long mefella, missis
My father is the chief of the Ralum warriors	Puppa belong me he luluai belong armi belong Ralum
I will look after you, madam	Me lookoutim you, missis
Do you have another cigarette, darling?	You got anatherfella kapstan, you leva belong me?
Yes, madam. I love you, madam	Yes, missis. Me like you too much, missis
Thank you, waiter	Tenk you, kukiboy
Goodbye, madam. Until tomorrow!	Goodbai, missis. Inuf tomorra!
Daphne! Bloody woman! Are you coming?	Dapne! Bladi mary! You likim come?
I'm coming, Nicholas	Me come-on, Nikas
It is raining again, Daphne	Rain he come-down gen, Dapne
I am getting drenched!	Rain he washim me!
Who first discovered New Guinea, Nicholas?	Who's-at he findim Nu Gini namba-wan time, Nikas?
Who cares!	Na kea!

NOTES (1933)

Good lad, he has used 'Bastet!' (Bastard) at last!

Now I know that Daphne is all for fraternising with the locals, but I don't hold with women smoking. Never have; call me old-fashioned if you will. <u>The natives smoke very strange substances</u>, which, in my opinion, has a good deal to do with their outrageous behaviour. They're a bit like the flies in the old sago, if you get my drift. (Will that be allowed in?)

I well remember my own first night at the Coconut Grove. We had round after round of native whisky. They call it medicine (medecin), but after that it all gets a bit fuzzy.

In those days they had native waitresses, don't know what's happened to them, with nothing on top – not a stitch – just grass skirts. Well, old 'Jumbo' decided to mow the lawn. Who would have thought a bit of fun would end up the way it did? I remember saying those very words to old 'Fish' in court the next day. He was worried about the heavy native casualties. Naturally, we were completely exonerated, though I will admit to being somewhat rattled by that piece in the Dagua Sosaiti News.

Funny thing, I never went back to the old C.G. again. 'Jumbo' did. He was always ready for a bit of slap and tickle, or, as we used to call it, 'clap and sickle'. He was an Old Harrovian, you know. Always wore the old school tie. Never without it. The cannibals cooked him in it, I believe. There was a saying in the club at the time: 'Old "Jumbo"? Ah, yes. Harrow and eaten.'

Poor old 'Jumbo'. Always did everybody harm.

Which reminds me that Nick and Daphne are still going to the highlands. I'm disappointed, I was hoping they'd change their minds. Could prove to be the most appalling blunder. I know what goes on up there, you see. I've been to a couple of battles myself. I'd be paddling past and was always invited to watch. It's rather like being transported back 4,000 years in a time machine. They still fight with bows and arrows, spears and axes (guns would be considered damned unsporting). To tell the truth, I found them to be the most charming people, but then I never met a hungry one. Trouble is, all that fighting gives them an appetite.

What they do is string their enemies up in the trees for later. A most unnerving sight. There's a whole ritual associated with it, which I won't go into now, but I've often wondered if this is where the expression 'He's well hung' came from.

The thing that was always uppermost in my mind was what would happen to me if they didn't have enough groceries for the post-battle party. I never stayed for the sing-sing. Old 'Ginger' did and went prematurely grey when he was offered Lady's Fingers and found that they were.

So you can understand my concern over this trip of Nick and Daphne's. Especially when I read that they're going up there to stay with a luluai (chief)! It's like Daniel and the lion's den. Whatever happened to him?

There is one other thing. I know this is going to sound like nitpicking, particularly in a moment of crisis, but I'm not very happy about Daphne taking that betelnut home. What does she think she's doing? Betelnut stains, and we all know she's prone to vomiting. I shudder to think what it does to the brain. Look at the locals. And she's got such lovely teeth. Well, she had such lovely teeth. God knows whose neck they're hanging round now.

RECOMMENDATION

Avoid chewing betelnut. This is quite easy to do.

RECOMMENDATION

Re nightclubs. The old Coconut Grove is hot, unpleasant and teeming with the little johnnies. It's very heavy on the pocket and I can't recommend it at all. That's my recommendation.
* One star and that's bloody generous.

In the '50s or so, some fellow wrote a book about the Ralum Massacre. He spelt my name Lotmeyer. Extraordinary.

I hadn't thought of it before, but these days they probably have credit cards in the jungle. I can have a bash at translating some of them for you, if you like, but I don't believe in them myself.

American Express	Kwik-kwik Belong Amerika
Master Charge	Unerarms Belong Masta
Diner's Club	Clob Belong Kai-kai
Visa	Plastik Belong Barklay Benk

Travelling by Aeroplane

GO LONG BALUS *

Is this where the aeroplane lands, Daphne?	Balus he fall-down disfella place, Dapne?
Yes, Nicholas	Yes, Nikas
How, Daphne?	All-same what-name, Dapne?
Why, Nicholas?	Belong what-name, Nikas?
It is a river, Daphne!	Him he wanfella riva, Dapne!
The aeroplane is a sea-plane, Nicholas	Balus he savvy sindown long water, Nikas
Are these natives waiting for the aeroplane, too?	All disfella kanaka he waitim long balus, too?
Yes, Nicholas. They are the Ralum army:	Yes, Nikas. All he stop armi belong Ralum:
the chief's son	pikinini man belong luluai
the driver	driva
the post office manager	bosboy belong post ofis
the bank manager	bosboy belong benk
the department store proprietor	bosboy belong bulk stor
the third man under the blanket	trifella man unerneat blanket
Hello, boys!	Halo, alla boy!
Hello, Daphne!	Halo, Dapne!
Good morning, madam!	Good moning, missis!
How are you, madam?	You orait, missis?
Hello, missis!	Halo, missis!
Hello, baby!	Halo, pikinini mary!

*Balus: Pidgin for 'bird'.

What are they carrying, Daphne?	What-name someting all carryim, Dapne?
Their uniforms, Nicholas	All klos belong armi belongim him, Nikas
Pots and baskets, Daphne?	All sospen en all baskit, Dapne?
They put the pots on their heads, and the baskets are for their balls and things, Nicholas	All putim all sospen long all hed belongim, en all baskit belong carryim all ball en all someting belongim him, Nikas
The plane! The plane!	Tu-wing! Tu-wing!
Boss, the plane is coming!	Bos, tu-wing he come now!
What are the natives singing, Daphne?	What-name someting all kanaka he sing-sing, Dapne?
I don't know, Nicholas. It sounds like *Drink To Me Only With Thine Eyes*	Aidono, Nikas. Itingk all he singout *Dringk Long Me Tas-all Wantime Long Eye Belong You*
Daphne, the aeroplane is an old bi-plane made of bits of timber!	Dapne, balus he oldfella tu-wing plank!
The pilot is mad!	Pailot he long-long!
The aeroplane is flying backwards and forwards!	Tu-wing he go, he come!
The plane has shaved off the top of the hill a bit!	Tu-wing he sharpim mounten lik-lik!
The bloody fool!	Bladiful!
The plane has shaved off the top of the church a bit!	Tu-wing he sharpim house loto lik-lik!
The aeroplane has shaved off the top of the Ritz Hotel a bit!	Tu-wing he sharpim Rits Hotel lik-lik!
Look out! The plane is landing!	Lookout! Tu-wing he fall-down!
The aeroplane is taking off!	Tu-wing he go on-top!
The plane is landing again!	Tu-wing he fall-down gen!

The plane has hit two . . .
three . . . four . . . five crocodiles!

Tu-wing he go-upim tu . . . tri
. . . fo . . . faiv puk-puk!

The plane has run over one
hundred crocodiles!

Tu-wing he go-upim wan handet
puk-puk!

ONE HUNDRED AND
EIGHTY!!

WAN HANDET HAITI!!

The aeroplane has bumped into
the bridge!

Tu-wing he bangim brids!

The pilot is shouting!

Pailot he singout!

Strewth! Thas the
***** king way ta do it!

By Jove! That is certainly
the way to do it!

Tru on-top! Asaway!

Me bloody landin's bloody
improvin', mate

I think my landing was a
little better, old chap

Itingk fall-down belong me
he moa betta, brada

Tough shit about the
***** king bridge

Pity about the bridge

Strongfella pek-pek long
brids

'Lo, cobbers! 'Ow
ya-goin'-awright?

Hello, everyone! And
how are we all?

Halo, alla frend! All
youfella orait?

Goin' up ta the hills for a
bitiva blue, boys?

So you're going to the
highlands for another
skirmish, are you, chaps?

Youfella by-en-by go long
mounten belong fight, alla
boy?

Yes, sir!
Indeed, sir!
Yes, sir!

Yesa!
Yesa!
Yesa!

Aw-bloody-right! Won't be
a sec

Righty-ho! I shan't be long

Bladi orait! Me come-back
kwik-kwik

Me bladder's bloody
burstin'!

Nature calls

Pis-pis belong me he
fire-up!

Godda hose down the
cassowary!

I must go behind a tree to
relieve myself!

Me must go wetim muruk!

Hop on the wing, fellas

All aboard, chaps

Come-up long wing,
allafella

Shit a possum! Me bloody fly buttons are buggered!	Oh deary me! All my buttons have come off!	Pek-pek wanfella cus-cus! All baton belong trousis belong me bugarup!
Daphne, the pilot is not mad; he is drunk		Dapne, pailot he no long-long; he spakman
Nicholas, the pilot is not mad or drunk; he is Orstralian		Nikas, pailot he no long-long o spakman; him he belong Ostrelya
Maybe all three, madam		Itingk he trifella, missis
The waiter says he's all three, Nicholas		Kukiboy tok pailot he trifella, Nikas
Now look here, you pilot-person –		Now look-look here, you pailot-man –
Shit a kangaroo! Who the ✳︎ ✳︎ ✳︎ *king hell are you?*	Well I never! And who, may I ask, are you?	Pek-pek wanfella kapul! Who's-at?
I am Nicholas Coffin of Ruislip		Me Nikas Coffin belong Rislip
Where the ✳︎ ✳︎ ✳︎ *king hell's that, cobber?*	And where would that be, my friend?	Rislip, where, brada?
Ruislip is a very important town in England		Rislip he namba-wan place long Inglan
Stone the crows! Who's the sheila?	Gracious! And who is the lady?	Olapukpuk! Who's-at mary?
I beg your pardon!		Me sory too much!
Why? Wocha do? Fart?	What for? What is it? Did you pass wind?	Watfor? What-name you makim someting? Belli he fire-up?
We want to buy a ticket to go to the highlands		Mefella like buyim tikit go long mounten on-top
Strike a light, mate! I don't sell bloody tickets!	My goodness, old chap! I'm not a ticket vendor!	Slekim machis, brada! Me no selim all bladi tikit!
I'm only the ✳︎ ✳︎ ✳︎ *king fline docker!*	Actually, I'm the flying doctor!	Me dokta belong flai, tas-all!
Good grief!		Goodfella sory!

You're a Pommy bastard, arncha, Nicky?	And you are from England, are you, Nicholas?	You belong Inglan, Niki?
Ya poor bugger! Grabba seat, cobber!	In that case I'll give you a lift, old son!	Me sory long you! You go inside long tu-wing!
Daphne, I can't understand a word this yobbo says!		Dapne, me no savvy tok belong disfella rabishman!
Hello, I'm Daphne Coffin. How are you?		Halo, me Dapne Coffin. You orait?
Bonzer, Daffy!	I'm splendid, Daphne!	Me orait, Dappy!
The name's Jack Hornbottle. Me friends call me Horny	My name is Jack Hornbottle. My nickname is Horners	Name belong me Jack Hornbotol. Frend belong me tok Horny
Fair dinkum, Nicky, thought yer old lady was a bloody boong in thad get up!	To tell the truth, Nicholas, I was under the impression that your lady wife, thus attired, had dropped out of the nearest tree!	Tru on-top, Niki, itingk cook belong you he all-same bush kanaka bikos long klos belong him!
Gone native, have you, love?	When in Rome, eh, Mrs Coffin?	You all-same kanaka, swit biskit?
Youra bitta awright, Daffy	What a little corker you are, Mrs Coffin	You orait, Dappy
Look like you'd be good in the sack!	I'd certainly like to mark your dance-card	You all-same mary he plenty goodfella long bet!
Thank you, Doctor Hornbottle		Tenk you, Dokta Hornbotol
I'm Horny, Daffy	Call me Horners, Daphne	Me Horny, Dappy
I say, you son of a convict!		Me tok, you pikinini man belong calabusman!
Take your hand off my wife's backside!		Takawayim han belong you long arse belong cook belong me!

Daphne, I'm getting into the plane now!		Dapne, me go inside tu-wing now!
Are you coming?		You come-on?
Good God, Doctor Hornbottle! The aeroplane is full of chickens		Good Got, Dokta Hornbotol! Tu-wing he full-up long all kakaruk!
And chicken droppings!		En pek-pek belong kakaruk!
Yeah, I know, Nicky. Dirty little buggers, aren't they?	Yes, indeed, Nicholas. They're far from house-trained, I'm afraid	Me savvy, Niki. Him he all doti smolfella, eh?
And the flies are the worst I've ever seen!		En all lang he moa no-good altagether me lookim alltime!
Don't be rude, Nicholas!		You no tok no-good, Nikas!
Doctor Hornbottle is going to mend them		Dokta Hornbotol he by-en-by sewim up
Daphne, I think you've gone mad! I will see you on the plane		Dapne, itingk you long-long! Me tok wantime long you long tu-wing
Stop here, Daffy. I wanna bitiva natter with ya	Do stay here, Daphne. I'd like a word in your ear	You stop here, Dappy. Me likim tok long you
Wozza madda with yer bedder half, Daffy?	What on earth could be the matter with your husband, Daphne?	Wasamarra wantime long man belong you, Dappy?
I don't know, Horny. I think he's hot		Aidono, Horny. Itingk he hot too much
I don't think he's so hot, Daffy!	I don't like the cut of his jib, Daphne!	Me no tingk he hot too much, Dappy!
Smoke, Daffy?	Would you care for a cigarette, Daphne?	You smok, Dappy?
Horny! You have native cigarettes!		Horny! You got all kapstan belong kanaka!

Yeah, they're beaudy bottlers, Daffy!	Yes, aren't they spiffing, Daphne!	Yes, all disfella he naisfella too much, Dappy!
Akshurly, the fellas pay me in ciggies, Daffy	Actually, the lads give them to me by way of recompense, Daphne	You savvy alla boy he payim me wantime long kapstan, Dappy
How will I pay you, Horny?		All-same what-name by-en-by me payim you, Horny?
Whada bouda —	Would you be interested in a —	All-same what —
Daphne! Bloody woman! No playing up now! Hurry up!		Dapne! Bladi mary! No can humbug now! Hariap!
Ratshit!	Bother!	Pek-pek belong rat!
Jeez, Daffy! Your old man's a real wowser!	Good Lord, Daphne! Your husband is a bit of a prig!	Yesus, Dappy! Oldfella man belong you all-same man belong misinary!
Wozza madder, Daffy? Wire ya limpin'?	What is the trouble, Daphne? Why are you limping?	Wasamarra, Dappy? Watfor you go kelap-kelap?
I have hurt my toe, Horny		Me bugarupim fingga belong fut belong me, Horny
I'll carrier, Daffy	I will carry you, Daphne	Me carryim you, Dappy
Yer wanna sid nexta me inna plane, Daffy?	Would you care to sit by me in the bi-plane, Daphne?	You likim sindown close-to me long tu-wing, Dappy?
I'll let yus drive	You might like to pilot the aircraft	By-en-by me larim you steerim
You've got real beaut norks, Daffy	That's a lovely blouse you have on, Daphne	You got naisfella susu, Dappy
Jesus! Look at that!	Good heavens! Don't look!	Yesus! Lookim disfella!
I'd bedder sew some bloody buddons on me bloody strides!	I shall have to sew some dashed buttons on these dashed trousers!	By-en-by me must sewimupim samfella baton long trousis belong me!

Okay! Yawl ready?	**Righty-ho! All set?**	Okei! Redi?
Here we go inta the wide blue yonda!	**Taking off now!**	You-me go now long bigfella heven he blufella!
Hang on!	**Hold tight!**	Holdimfast!
Crocs away!	**That's just silly**	Goodbai all puk-puk!
Geta loada this, Daffy	**Watch this, Daphne**	You lookim, Dappy
Shit a missionary! I hit another bloody tree!	**Oh dear! I just scraped another tree!**	Pek-pek wanfella misinary! Me go-upim anatherfella tri!
What's up, Daffy? You crook?	**What ails you, Daphne? Are you ill?**	Wasamarra, Dappy? You feelim no-good?
You wanta chunder, love?	**You're not going to do anything silly, are you, dearest?**	.You likim throw-out, swit biskit?
She'll be apples!	**You'll be fine in no time at all!**	By-en-by him he moa betta!
Hava beer, Daffy	**Would you care for a lager, Daphne?**	You likim wanfella beer, Dappy?
That'll put hair on yer chest!	**It will settle your stomach**	By-en-by him he putim grass long susu belong you
Givus a beer, too, willya Daff?	**May I have a lager, too, Daphne?**	Gisim wanfella beer, Dapp
I wanna wed me whistle	**My throat is dry**	Me likim wet nek belong me
Ya tummy rumblin', love?	**Feeling peckish, my dear?**	You hangre, swit biskit?
The boys made me some bonzer yam sannitches	**The chaps ran up some super yam sandwiches for me**	Alla boy he makim me samfella senwits mami he goodfella
Anda cassowary hamburga	**Also a game rissole**	En wanfella slais muruk he fryim
Wife! Are you drinking again?		Cook belong me! You dringk wantime moa?
My God! You are both drinking!		Got Belong Me! All you tufella dringk!

Fancy a squirt, do you, mate?	You feel like having a drink with us, old chap?	You likim dringk, brada?
You Jezebel!		You Jezebel all-same Jezebel long Bibol!
Don't shout, Nicholas		You no big-mousen, Nikas
Shut up, wife!		Tok him die finish, cook belong me!
Sidown mate or I'll belt ya one!	Sit down, old chap, or I may be obliged to use force!	Sindown, frend, o suppos you no sindown me hitim you long hed belong you!
Goodness gracious! What is that thing, pilot?		Olapukpuk! What-name someting belong him?
Me flies are buggered, that's all, ya fartass!	There are a few buttons off my trews, you flatulent fool!	Trousis belong me he bugarup, tas-all, windim arse!
You bastard! You've seduced my wife!		Bastet! You makim frend long cook belong me!
Givus a chance!	Not yet!	No got!
Sit down, Nicholas, and keep quiet!		Sindown, Nikas, en fastin mouse!
I can't, Daphne		No can, Dapne
There are chicken droppings all over my backside!		He got pek-pek belong kakaruk coverupim arse belong me!
Shit! Did yous hear that?	Oh dear! Did you hear that?	Pek-pek! You hearim disfella?
The bloody engine's buggered!	The rotten old engine's missing!	Bladi mashin he fire-up!
Horny, the engine's on fire!		Horny, mashin he fire!
Shit a rabbi!	This is worse than I thought!	Pek-pek wanfella pater long seminari!
Hey, boys! Put out the fire! Hose the old cassowary!	Come on, lads! Fire drill! Improvise!	Hey, alla boy! Makim die fire! Wetim oldfella muruk!

*Jeez, the ✳ * *✳ king engine's fallen off now!*	Hello, there goes the engine!	Yesus, bladi mashin he fall-down now!
The plane is crashing, Horny!		Tu-wing he bugarup, Horny!
Shit a cathedral!	Holy shit!	Pek-pek wanfella house lotu belong bisop!
Oh Horny, my darling, what shall we do?		O Horny, you swit biskit, what-name you-me makim someting?
Fark me, Daffy!	I don't know what I'm meant to do here!	Aidono, Dappy!

NOTES (1 APRIL 1934)

Of course, you can't tell from reading it, but this chapter arrived in Ruislip three months after the others and during that time there was no word from them at all. A very worrying time, I can tell you. I've been like a bear with a sore head. Mrs P. has threatened to leave on more than one occasion. Here I was in Mafeking Avenue, thinking I'd sent them up to the highlands to be eaten by cannibals. Thank goodness the aeroplane crashed, that's all I can say. I've never approved of it: flying, I mean. If God had meant us to fly, he'd have given us propellers.

Anyway, it all arrived yesterday and now, at least, I know they're alive. Well, Daphne is. They both certainly survived the crash.

As well as the manuscript there were two separate letters and several sketches, which I thought you might like to see. The letters are self-explanatory and very confusing.

What on earth has happened to Daphne? Is it Daphne on the boat to Samoa? If not, who is masquerading as a Coffin? Where is Nicholas? Who is the mysterious person with blitzed hair? Why are they sailing to Samoa? Are they ever going to finish the Pisin phrasebook?

I don't know what to do now. Should I continue with my 'Notes'? My heart's not in it any more.

My dear Major Latymer,

Today we had a stroke of bad luck, I'm afraid. The bi-plane in which we were travelling to the highlands caught fire and now we are stranded in the jungle.

Nicholas, who, as you know, has a very short fuse, is not behaving well at all.

After the crash I was, naturally, continuing my work on the phrasebook when he suddenly attacked me, struck me and threw my new notebook into the river where, unfortunately, it was eaten by crocodiles. He averred that I should have been making a home for us and busying myself in the kitchen rather than, as he put it, 'scribbling boring conversations in a Pisin phrasebook'.

This, as it turned out, was all quite unnecessary, as we are not alone. By happy happenstance, the Ralum warriors were travelling to a fighting engagement in the highlands on the same bi-plane as ourselves, and they are six very charming, very helpful young men, whose resourcefulness in our present situation has been boundless. They have worked miracles of ingenuity under the inspired leadership of our pilot, Dr John Hornbottle: one of the most remarkable men I have ever met.

The boys have already created an extremely comfortable shelter* from the wreckage of the aeroplane and, even as I write, they are now preparing what smells like a most delicious meal for this evening. Such is our state of civilisation that I have been asked to write on the other side of this page so they can use our very last sheet of writing paper for making out a menu for our evening meal!

So, as you can see, dear Major, I am being looked after in a most excellent manner and I am writing this in the hope that, by some

---

*The third man under the blanket has just handed me a torn piece of paper he found in the wreckage so, dear Major, I will be able to include a drawing of their splendid erection.

P.T.O.

serendipity, one day this letter will reach you in Ruislip and you will
then understand why our next chapters failed to arrive on your doorstep.

Nicholas, reluctantly I admit, has been dragged off to help with
the meal, but I am sure he would want to send his regards to you and
join me in avowing that our first task on returning to the outside
world will be to purchase a new notebook and resume our work on the
'Conversational Beginner's Phrasebook of Pidgin-English'.

Until then, my dear Major, I remain

Your devoted

Daphne

Daphne (Coffin)

P.S. How is Mrs P?

MENU

11 OCTOBER 1933

DINNER

TU BOL à l'ANGLAISE

GRILLED LIZARD
OR
BOILED BAT

CRUSHED CASSOWARY
IN
TREE TRUNK
OR
MASHED BIRD OF PARADISE
WITH
MINCED YAM
AND
PIECES OF PROPELLER

A MÉLANGE OF
TROPICAL FRUIT

Hello Shuthouse,

Who are you, you old bigger?"**

Windy Grenn here.

Remember me? I'm captain of Thr Queem of Thr Sea. I thinj.

Quite a surpride, eh, Shotty! Dont write mamy letters. Weel, none of my wibes can bloddy read can they%¼? Still got the shakes old bot. Writings still as bad as eber but now I use this typewroter..., I got it from an authir fellow. He got veru drunk, feel overboard and left it behind***/?½ I sit happily foe hours with my botttle tryimg to find thr bloody keya. You know old mam, I thinj it's bettter than a bloddy woman. Its got a belll too⅓½?!

Well hereres to you Shutty...£

Hers to you again you olf sjitgousa%⅓½"

Wrote that last night old chap. Thinj I was a bit pisssed.,½

Look you silly oldbuger, Id' almost forgotten you until yersterdat, then something very stramge happened,;.

I'll start at the begimmimg,*-

I had this passenget on board on my lasr trip from somewhere, a bliddy awful english womam called Coffin. She only turned uk with a blackman -&"? (with <u>blitzed</u> hair!!?) Thought I had thr D.Ts when I spitted him.

Anyway old coci. Im in my cabim most of the time as I've decided to writr my life story -"/(These daya Im drunking to rememember⅓½"?) so I didnt see much of then;:.

Howeber,, today we sailed into whererever we are now and it turns out the pair of then have run up considererable bar bills and cant pay then.

Weel,, this womam marches into my cabim and in leiu of payment gives me this bumdle of pappers addresssed to <u>you</u> old mam?-+! I was shocked I can telll you. Zhe said shez writong a bookk qith you??!½

She doesn't look like your type Shotty. She doesmt look like my type either.. I can(t abibe mousoustachioed womem. Remind me of my moter*@/!

I thinj I need a drimk. Cheeers$\frac{37}{68}$!

Where was i! She gives me the package and saya I will be weel rewarded for sending it off to you,. Is she stark roving bankers old chap!?

I would'nt mind a bit of a windfalll. Wives are very ezpensive. You should seee my last one$\frac{1}{2}$. I should see my last one but I c'ant rememember which port shes' in.

Hereres to you old chap+=! The sun's just come over thr pothole.

About that money, If therere is any could you send it to me care ob Burns Phillilip I think. it is%:@℃£££?

They werere good old days, Shittty ole thinh. A lot of drink haz flowed under my bridge xince then.

Who is your foot or is it your hanc-!*? I know the litttle buggera ate somethint of yours.

The'yve still got my ear -., yes my ear..

Cheeers shotty old mam. Hang on i have to get anither bittle.

Hello Shighouwe old budddy!**??

Send thr bloddy money quick will you olf mam-?

I thinj I misss you Zhitty.

Keepp taking thr medecine

Your fellow autjor,

Willliam. P. Green

(Wondy to you$\frac{1}{4}$)

P.S. Got one of my boys to rake out a phototogralh of thr autyor at worm. A photographet got drink fell ovetboqrd and levt his canera behind,.

PP.S. Seeen anuthing of "*!- can't rember names - Scrubby or was ir Pigggy:$\frac{1}{3}$?

P.P.P.S. Hereres who old mam@@&'(($\frac{3}{4}$

I remember I mounted an expedition to look for them in '36 or '37 but something happened and it was cancelled. Then I tried again – in '38, I think it was. Mrs P. tells me it was '39 and she's quite right: the War intervened and in the end the expedition never materialised.

Neither did Daphne and Nicholas.

An extraordinary thing happened a few years later. Old 'Foggy', who lives around the corner and knew the Coffins, caused an awful fuss because he thought he'd found a photograph of Daphne in a National Geographic Magazine. That blasted photograph did the rounds of Ruislip. Mrs P. caught up with it at the butcher's and carried it home in triumph. It was a picture of a native woman in the wilds of New Guinea who happened to be called 'Missis Kwin Dapne' (Queen Daphne). Well, Ruislip needed no more. The whole place went berserk for days. Mrs P. was Queen of the May (Mrs Kwin Belong Namba-faiv Moon) and held court in the kitchen. Never seen so much tea in my life. And all over this picture.

Now I'll swear it wasn't our Daphne. For one thing, she didn't have any clothes on, but 'Foggy', Mrs P. and the whole population of Ruislip were convinced that it was.

I don't know how they thought they could tell. I have never seen Daphne without her clothes on in my life and I hope I never do. I don't think I would recognise anyone I know without his clothes, except old 'Windy', of course, and that's only because he has a beard and one ear. Cut off his head and I wouldn't have a clue who he was.

'Missis Kwin Dapne' (Queen Daphne) captured here holding court in the wilds of New Britain.

Funny about old 'Windy', wasn't it? The book*, I mean. He didn't get my name right, either. Spelt it Latymoz. Silly old fool.

Where was I? I keep drifting off these days.

The thing is, Mrs P. says that the photograph is evidence and has to be included, but I think she reads too many detective stories and, just between you and me, her eyesight's been dreadful for years and she won't wear her spectacles.

However, there's something else that's even more puzzling about the whole affair. It's all very difficult. You see, someone did mention having seen Nicholas at the Hotel Australia in Sydney in 1934. Someone else claims to have seen him in a rickshaw in Hong Kong in '35. Someone else saw him outside a pyramid in Cairo in '37, or was it a cinema? And then he was spotted being escorted from the Casino in Monte. Then old 'Humbug' went into the Montreux Clinic to dry out one Lent (Mrs P. maintains, mysteriously, that it was more to do with opium), and he swears he saw Nick there. In his excitement, he borrowed someone's camera and took a perfectly good photograph of his own stomach.

I know all this because Mrs P. has documented every single sighting.

'Humbug''s sighting was in 1937. Then in 1938 Nick was seen on the Ile de France. (Mrs P. has marked this down as a 'definite sighting'.) Mrs Luciano from the greengrocer's went to New York to see her cousins. There's a very poor quality snapshot stuck beside this information. I'm not surprised; old Mrs Luciano never understood anything. (I don't honestly see how she can call this a 'definite sighting'.)

Somehow, in '39, Nicholas returned to Europe, because he was again photographed, again badly, on the terrace of the Adler Hotel in Berlin.

There were no sightings during the War, which was a great disappointment to Mrs P. However, shortly afterwards I received a photograph from Rio. Our old butcher had sent it. He did very well for himself during rationing and subsequently became an importer. He also knew Daphne – I'm not sure if he knew Nick – but at least he seemed to know what he was doing with a camera.

I can't think how to put the next bit. I knew I'd regret starting this. The point is, all these reports said that Nicholas had turned into a woman. It's nonsense of course, don't you think? I mean, I know young Nick and that sort of thing doesn't happen to people one knows, does it? Not even very often to people one doesn't know.

Anyway, over the next few years it all fizzled out rather. Rationing, rebuilding and the Labour Party took over as the main topics of conversation, and the Coffins were forgotten.

Almost. In 1953 there was an article about them in the Ruislip and Ickenham Advertiser to celebrate the twentieth anniversary of their disappearance. I'm not going to include it because Mrs P.'s nephew wrote it and spelt my name wrongly yet again and, anyway, it was only snippets from the above (except for that part about Nicholas being a woman).

(I'm all for cutting that out, you know. If he should read this, he might well have me up for slander, or the other thing.)

*William P. Green's book, Plastered In Paradise, was a best-selling autobiographical novel in 1937.

Hepi Krismas,
Dear Major!

126

I nearly forgot the Christmas card. Mrs P. says it's conclusive proof, but I think she's becoming a bit silly in her old age. It arrived some years after the War and was postmarked Rabaul. Still, that's hardly conclusive, is it? I know a great many people in New Guinea and, to tell the truth, it looks more like Dirty Mary (Doti Mary) to me.

However, I've put it in the bundle. I'm a bit like Neville Chamberlain these days. Anything for peace.

> Place belong me he namba-wan,
> Me likim him tas-all.

127